Mike Ruth 3.50

P9-CKV-526

Be
Ready

Warren W. Wiersbe

This book is designed for your personal
reading pleasure and profit. It is also designed for group study. A leader's guide
with helps and hints for teachers and
visual aids (Victor Multiuse Transparency
Masters) is available from your local book-
store or from the publisher at $2.95.

VICTOR BOOKS

a division of SP Publications, Inc.
WHEATON, ILLINOIS 60187

Offices also in Fullerton, California • Whitby, Ontario, Canada • Amersham-on-the-Hill, Bucks, England

Fifth printing, 1981

Most of the Scripture quotations in this book are
from the King James Version (KJV). Other quotations are from *The New International Version:
New Testament* (NIV), © 1973 by The New York
Bible Society; the *New American Standard Bible*
(NASB), © 1960, 1962, 1963, 1968, 1971, 1973 by
the Lockman Foundation, La Habra, California;
The New Testament in Modern English (PH),
© 1958, by J.B. Phillips, The Macmillan Company;
and the *Revised Standard Version* (RSV), © 1946
and 1952, the Division of Christian Education,
National Council of Churches of Christ in the
U.S.A.

Recommended Dewey Decimal Classification: 227.81
    Suggested Subject Headings: BIBLE, N.T. 1 AND 2 THES-
    SALONIANS

Library of Congress Catalog Card Number: 78-65555
ISBN: 0-88207-782-1

© 1979 by SP Publications, Inc. All rights reserved
Printed in the United States of America

VICTOR BOOKS
A division of SP Publications, Inc.
P.O. Box 1825 • Wheaton, Illinois 60187

Contents

Dedicated with appreciation
to friends whose ministry
was above and beyond the call of duty:

Lee and Claudia Gerwin
Gareth and Bev Nelson
Evelyn Rankin
Carol Thiessen

Preface

The two major themes in 1 and 2 Thessalonians are dear to my heart: the return of Jesus Christ and the ministry of the local church.

In these two letters, Paul balances the prophetical and the practical. He insists that the doctrine of the return of Jesus Christ be more than a doctrine—that it be a dynamic in our lives and in the ministry of our churches.

This is the seventh book in the BE series. I want to thank Henry Jacobsen, who got the series started, and James Adair, Editorial Director of Victor Books, who encourages me to keep it going.

Christ is coming soon. BE READY!

Warren W. Wiersbe

¹Now when they had passed through Amphipolis and Apollonia, they came to Thessalonica, where was a synagogue of the Jews: ²and Paul, as his manner was, went in unto them, and three Sabbath Days reasoned with them out of the Scriptures, ³opening and alleging, that Christ must needs have suffered, and risen again from the dead; "and that this Jesus, whom I preach unto you, is Christ." ⁴And some of them believed, and consorted with Paul and Silas; and of the devout Greeks a great multitude, and of the chief women not a few. ⁵But the Jews which believed not, moved with envy, took unto them certain lewd fellows of the baser sort, and gathered a company, and set all the city on an uproar, and assaulted the house of Jason, and sought to bring them out to the people. ⁶And when they found them not, they drew Jason and certain brethren unto the rulers of the city, crying, "These that have turned the world upside down are come hither also; ⁷whom Jason hath received: and these all do contrary to the decrees of Caesar, saying that there is another king, one Jesus." ⁸And they troubled the people and the rulers of the city, when they heard these things. ⁹And when they had taken security of Jason, and of the other, they let them go. ¹⁰And the brethren immediately sent away Paul and Silas by night unto Berea: who coming thither went into the synagogue of the Jews.

¹¹These were more noble than those in Thessalonica, in that they received the Word with all readiness of mind, and searched the Scriptures daily, whether those things were so. ¹²Therefore many of them believed; also of honorable women which were Greeks, and of men, not a few. ¹³But when the Jews of Thessalonica had knowledge that the Word of God was preached of Paul at Berea, they came thither also, and stirred up the people. ¹⁴And then immediately the brethren sent away Paul to go as it were to the sea: but Silas and Timotheus abode there still. ¹⁵And they that conducted Paul brought him unto Athens: and receiving a commandment unto Silas and Timotheus for to come to him with all speed, they departed.

Acts 17:1-15

Paul, and Silvanus, and Timotheus, unto the church of the Thessalonians which is in God the Father and in the Lord Jesus Christ: Grace be unto you, and peace, from God our Father, and the Lord Jesus Christ.

1 Thessalonians 1:1

1
A Church Is Born

A father took his son to a large city museum, thinking that the visit would entertain the boy. But for two hours the lad did nothing but sigh and complain. Finally in desperation he said to his father, "Dad, let's go someplace where *things are real!*"

Some people feel that way when they read the Bible. They think they are in a religious museum, looking at ancient artifacts that have no meaning for life in today's scientific world. *But they are wrong.* No book published has more meaning for our lives, and more relevance to our problems, than the Bible. No wonder William Lyon Phelps, for years called "Yale's most inspiring professor," said: "I believe a knowledge of the Bible without a college course is more valuable than a college course without a Bible."

We are about to study two of Paul's earliest letters, 1 and 2 Thessalonians. (It is possible that Galatians was written first.) These two letters were written to real people who were experiencing real problems in a world that was not friendly to their

Christian faith. You and I can easily identify with these people because we live in a similar world and face many of the same problems. Once you understand the background, the burden, and the blessing of these two letters, you will see how up-to-date and practical they are.

The Background

You can visit Thessalonica today, only the travel guide will call it Thessaloniki. (It used to be known as Salonika.) It is an important industrial and commercial city in modern Greece and is second to Athens in population. It served as an important Allied base during World War I. In World War II it was captured by the German army, and the Jewish population of about 60,000 persons was deported and exterminated.

It is an ancient city, originally named Therma from the many hot springs adjacent to it. In 315 B.C. it was renamed Thessalonica after the half sister of Alexander the Great. When Rome conquered Macedonia in 168 B.C., the city was made capital of that entire province. In Paul's day 200,000 people lived there, most of them Greeks, but also many Romans and a strong Jewish minority. Today it has a population of 300,000, and is one of the few cities that has survived from the New Testament era of apostolic ministry.

Dr. Luke explained how Paul came to Thessalonica and how the church was founded (Acts 17:1-15). Paul went to Macedonia in response to a "call" from a man in Macedonia who said, "Come over into Macedonia and help us" (Acts 16:9). Paul, Silas, Luke, and Timothy arrived first in Philippi where they led Lydia and her household to Christ and there established a church. Paul and

Silas were arrested on false charges, beaten, and put into jail. But God delivered them and they were able to lead the jailer and his household to faith in Christ.

After encouraging the new believers, Paul and his friends left Philippi (though Luke probably stayed behind temporarily) and headed for the important city of Thessalonica. They bypassed Amphipolis and Apollonia (Acts 17:1), not because they had no burden for the people in those cities, but because Paul's policy was to minister in the large cities and then have the believers reach out into the smaller towns nearby. It is about 100 miles from Philippi to Thessalonica.

Paul's commission was to take the Gospel to the Gentiles (Acts 9:15; Ephesians 3:1-12), but he always started his ministry among the Jews. The local synagogue was the place where the Old Testament Law was known and revered. Paul could get a sympathetic hearing in the synagogue, at least until persecution began. Furthermore, there were always many Gentile "God-fearers" in the synagogues, and through them Paul could begin a witness to the pagan Gentiles. Add to this Paul's great burden for the Jews (Romans 9:1-3 and 10:1), and the historical principle of "To the Jew first" (Rom. 1:16), and you can see why Paul and his associates began their work in the synagogue.

It is interesting to study the words Luke used to describe Paul's public ministry in the synagogue (Acts 17:2-3). *Reasoned* means "to discourse using questions and answers." Perhaps "dialogue" would be a good synonym. *Opening* simply means "explaining." Paul would read a portion of the Old Testament Scriptures and explain their meaning with reference to Jesus Christ and the Gospel.

Alleging literally means "to lay beside." Paul put the Scriptures before them in an orderly manner, showing them how they harmonized. *Preach* means "to proclaim, to announce." Paul did not simply teach the Scriptures; he proclaimed Christ and urged his listeners to receive Him by faith.

We can learn much from Paul's approach to evangelism. He used the Word of God, and he declared the Son of God. He started where the people were and led them into the truth of the Gospel. (When Paul preached to Gentiles, he started with the God of Creation, since they had no knowledge of the Old Testament Scriptures. See Acts 14:8-18 and 17:16ff.)

He ministered in the synagogue for three Sabbaths, and the Lord worked in power. Many people believed in Jesus Christ and were saved, including a number of high-ranking women. However, the unbelieving Jews began to oppose the work, and Paul and his helpers had to leave the city. They went 40 miles to Berea and there had a good ministry; but the Jews from Thessalonica followed them and caused trouble. It was then that Paul left for Athens, and from there to Corinth.

How long did Paul minister in Thessalonica? Does the statement "three Sabbath days" (Acts 17:2) mean three weeks only, or that he preached *in the synagogue* only three weeks but continued in another place? We know that Paul was there long enough to receive two "home missions offerings" from the church in Philippi (Phil. 4:16). Also, Paul worked at his tentmaking trade to support himself (1 Thes. 2:9 and 2 Thes. 3:6-15).

If Paul were there only three weeks, he certainly taught the new Christians a great deal of basic Bible doctrine. As we study these two letters, we will discover that almost every major doctrine of the Christian faith is mentioned.

Even though Paul's ministry in Thessalonica was not a long one, it was solid enough to leave behind a thriving church. When he left for Athens, Paul told Timothy and Silas to remain there and help the new church and then to join him later. When they did meet again, Paul sent Timothy back to Thessalonica to encourage the Christians and assure them of his love and concern. (He had tried to go back twice, but was hindered; 1 Thes. 2:17-18.) It was when Timothy rejoined Paul at Corinth and gave him the report on the new church that Paul wrote 1 Thessalonians. He wrote 2 Thessalonians just a short time later.

All of this background teaches us several helpful lessons. Obviously, *God uses people*. God did not send angels to evangelize Thessalonica; He sent a converted Jewish rabbi and his friends, including a young man who was part Jew, part Gentile. God still uses people—dedicated people who will obey His leading and share His message.

Here is a second lesson: the Gospel is still "the power of God unto salvation" (Rom. 1:16). It did not require years to set up a church in Thessalonica. God's power was effective in changing lives and a church was founded in less than a month. Paul reminded them that the Gospel came to them not "in word only, but also in power in the Holy Spirit" (1 Thes. 1:5).

Finally, Satan still opposes the Gospel and persecutes God's people; *but persecution can be a means of growth*. As we study these two letters, we will see that God's Spirit strengthens and encourages suffering saints as they go through the difficulties of Christian life and witness.

The Burden

Why did Paul write these two letters? First, he wanted to assure his friends of his love and concern. After all, he left the city hastily at night, and he did not want them to think he had deserted them. Also, Paul's enemies were attacking his character and telling the new believers that their leader was really a greedy charlatan who preached religion in order to make money (1 Thes. 2). There were plenty of itinerant rogues in Greece who did just that, and some were spreading the word that Paul was one of them. In this letter, Paul assured his readers of his love for them and his honesty in ministering to them.

He had a second purpose in view: he wanted to ground them in the doctrines of the Christian faith, particularly with reference to Christ's return. It appears that the church was going through severe persecution, and this is always a time of temptation to compromise and give in to discouragement. By reminding them of the truths of the Christian faith and what God had done for them in Christ, Paul encouraged them to stand firm and maintain their strong witness.

He also encouraged them to live holy lives. Keep in mind that temptations to immorality were rife in the cities then, and that sexual sins were not condemned by most people. These letters emphasize purity of life—a concept that needs to be emphasized in our churches too.

The new Christians were confused about the return of Jesus Christ. Paul had told them that the Lord would return in the air and take them home, but some of their number had died. The bereaved ones wondered if their Christian dead would be included in the "catching up" of the church. Paul explained this in 1 Thessalonians 4:13-18.

But there was a second confusion. Because the persecutions were so intense, some of the believers thought that "the Day of the Lord" had arrived. (It is possible that a forged letter contributed to this confusion. See 2 Thes. 2:1-2.) Paul wrote 2 Thessalonians to explain this doctrine and to assure them that the Day of the Lord had not yet arrived.

Finally, in this letter, Paul sought to correct some weaknesses in the church. Some members were not respecting and honoring their spiritual leaders as they should (1 Thes. 5:12-13). Others were refusing to work, arguing that the soon-coming of the Lord made this the logical thing to do (2 Thes. 3:6ff.). There was some confusion in their public services that also needed correcting (1 Thes. 5:19-21).

Confusion still exists about Bible prophecy, with radio and television preachers contradicting each other (and the Bible) and upsetting the saints. Is the coming of the Lord near? Must any signs take place before He can return? Will God's people have to go through the Day of the Lord (the tribulation) before He can return? Paul answered these important questions in these two inspired letters.

And what about the matter of *practical holiness?* It is not easy for Christians to avoid the pollutions of the world. The sex promoters offer their wares at almost every newspaper stand and drug store. Immorality and infidelity are common themes of radio and television programs as well as of popular music. The bad examples of famous people make it easier for young people to say, "Everybody is doing it!"

In addition to being more cautious in daily living, we also need more order and respect in our local churches. I have discovered that lack of respect for spiritual leadership is the main cause of church fights and splits. What Paul wrote in 1 Thessalonians 5:12-13 and 2 Thessalonians 3:6-15 is greatly needed today.

In all fairness to church officers, I realize that some pastors do not deserve to be followed. They are not spiritual; they do not pray; and they have no concern for the lost. They are merely using the ministry to make an easy living. A pastor must not *demand* respect; he must *command* respect, as did Paul, by his dedicated life and sacrificial ministry.

First Thessalonians is a letter from a spiritual father to his children. Paul pictured the church as a family (the word "brethren" or "brother" is used 19 times in the first letter and 9 times in the second), and he reminded them of what God did for them through his ministry. From this viewpoint, an outline of 1 Thessalonians would look like this:

I. PAUL REMEMBERS—chapters 1—3
   1. How the church was born—chapter 1
   2. How the church was nurtured—chapter 2
   3. How the church was established—chapter 3
II. PAUL EXHORTS—chapters 4—5
(How the church should walk)
   1. In holiness—4:1-8
   2. In harmony—4:9-10
   3. In honesty—4:11-12
   4. In hope—4:13—5:11
   5. In helpfulness—5:12-28

The second letter was written to correct certain

wrong ideas—and wrong practices—relating to the doctrine of the Lord's return. We will deal with the details of this letter in later chapters; but for now, a simple outline of 2 Thessalonians will be helpful:

I. ENCOURAGEMENT IN SUFFERING—chapter 1
  1. Praise—1:1-4
  2. Promise—1:5-10
  3. Prayer—1:11-12

II. ENLIGHTENMENT IN TEACHING—chapter 2
  1. How the man of sin appears—2:1-7
  2. How the Son of God appears—2:8-12
  3. How the child of God should live—2:13-17

III. ENABLEMENT IN LIVING—chapter 3
  1. Obey the Word—3:1-6
  2. Follow our example—3:7-9
  3. Discipline the unruly—3:10-15
  4. Closing benediction—3:16-18

We have seen the background of the letters, and the burden that motivated Paul to write them. We shall now consider the blessing of these letters and discover what they can mean to us.

The Blessing

Each New Testament letter has a special message, or blessing, that is uniquely its own. Romans, for example, emphasizes the righteousness of God and shows that God is righteous in His dealings with both sinners and believers. First Corinthians focuses on the wisdom of God, and 2 Corinthians on the comfort of God. Galatians is the freedom letter and Philippians is the joy letter, while Ephesians stresses the wealth that we have in Christ Jesus.

What is the special blessing in the message of 1 and 2 Thessalonians? *It is the message of the return of Jesus Christ and how this vital doctrine can affect our lives and churches and make us more spiritual.* Every chapter in 1 Thessalonians ends with reference to the coming of Jesus Christ, and each reference relates the doctrine to a practical aspect of Christian living. Here is a summary:

> 1:10—salvation and assurance
> 2:19-20—soul-winning and service
> 3:11-13—stability in Christian living
> 4:13-18—strength for sorrow
> 5:23-24—sanctification of life

In other words, Paul did not look on this doctrine as a theory to be discussed, but as a truth to be lived. These letters encourage us to live "in the future tense" since Jesus could appear at any time. We are to practice the promise of His return in our manner of life.

Turning to 2 Thessalonians, we discover additional truth concerning future events and the church. Keep in mind that the second letter was written to correct the confusion regarding our Lord's return. Some believers thought the Day of the Lord (the time of tribulation) had arrived, and they wondered when the Lord would appear. Perhaps the best way to grasp the major messages of the two letters is by contrast:

1 THESSALONIANS	2 THESSALONIANS
Christ comes in the air for His church (4:13-18)	Christ comes to the earth with His church (1:10)

A sudden secret rapture that can occur at any time	A crisis that is part of a predicted program
Can occur today	Can occur only after certain events happen
The Day of Christ	The Day of the Lord

I realize that godly men differ in their interpretations of prophecy, particularly the matter of the church escaping or entering the time of Tribulation. My own position is that the church will be taken to heaven before the Tribulation, and then will return to the earth with the Lord to bring the Tribulation to a close (Rev. 19:11ff.). I see 1 Thessalonians emphasizing the rapture of the church and 2 Thessalonians the revelation of the Lord with the church when He comes to judge.

However, the practical spiritual lessons of these truths should not be lost in debates over interpretations. I am encouraged to read what Dr. Leon Morris wrote in his excellent commentary on the Thessalonian epistles in *The New International Commentary* (Eerdmans, 1959), p. 152.

In his discussion of 1 Thessalonians 5:1-3, Dr. Morris faced the matter of whether believers will escape the Tribulation or be left on earth to pass through that terrible event. "The language of this chapter could be understood either way," he stated, and then affirmed his own position that the church will go through the tribulation. Then he added: "But I fully recognize that other interpretations are possible, and suggest that it is not wise for any of us to condemn those who see such passages differently."

In other words, we can disagree without being

disagreeable. My own conviction is that we shall be delivered from "the wrath to come" (1 Thes. 1:10 and 5:9-10). I believe the Lord wants us to live in the constant expectation of His coming. I have studied carefully the excellent defenses of the other positions, and I respect the men who hold to them. But I must lovingly disagree with them.

Paul did not write these letters to stir up a debate. His desire was that these letters bless our lives and our churches. The doctrine of the Lord's return is not a toy to play with, or a weapon to fight with, but a tool to build with. Believers may disagree on some of the fine points of Bible prophecy, but we all believe that Jesus Christ is coming again to reward believers and judge the lost. And we must all live in the light of His coming.

Your study of these letters should give you assurance for the future, encouragement in witnessing and walking with the Lord, comfort in the loss of Christian loved ones, and stability in a world that is very unsure of itself. Practicing what Paul wrote in these two letters should help you to BE READY!

¹Paul, and Silvanus, and Timotheus, unto the church of the Thessalonians which is in God the Father and in the Lord Jesus Christ; Grace be unto you, and peace, from God our Father, and the Lord Jesus Christ. ²We give thanks to God always for you all, making mention of you in our prayers; ³remembering without ceasing your work of faith, and labor of love, and patience of hope in our Lord Jesus Christ, in the sight of God and our Father; ⁴knowing, brethren beloved, your election of God. ⁵For our Gospel came not unto you in word only, but also in power, and in the Holy Ghost, and in much assurance; as ye know what manner of men we were among you for your sake. ⁶And ye became followers of us, and of the Lord, having received the word in much affliction, with joy of the Holy Ghost; ⁷so that ye were examples to all that believe in Macedonia and Achaia. ⁸For from you sounded out the Word of the Lord not only in Macedonia and Achaia, but also in every place your faith to God-ward is spread abroad; so that we need not to speak any thing. ⁹For they themselves show of us what manner of entering in we had unto you, and how ye turned to God from idols to serve the living and true God; ¹⁰and to wait for His Son from heaven, whom He raised from the dead, even Jesus, which delivered us from the wrath to come.

1 Thessalonians 1:1-10

2

What Every Church Should Be

No doubt you have heard some preacher say, "If you ever find the perfect church, *please don't join it*. If you do, it won't be perfect any more!"

Since local churches are made up of human beings, saved by God's grace, no church is perfect. But some churches are closer to the New Testament ideal than others. The church at Thessalonica was in that category. At least four times in this letter, Paul gave thanks for the church and the way it responded to his ministry (1:2; 2:13; 3:9; 5:18). Not every pastor can be that thankful.

What characteristics of this church made it so ideal and such a joy to Paul's heart?

An Elect People (1:1-4)
The word *church* in verse 1 means "a called-out people." Whenever you read about a *call* in the Bible, it indicates divine election—God is calling out a people from this world (Acts 15:13-18). Seven times in John 17, our Lord referred to believers as those whom the Father gave to Him out

of the world (2, 6, 9, 11, 12, 24). Paul stated that he knew the Thessalonians had been chosen by God (1:4).

The doctrine of divine election confuses some people and frightens others, yet neither response is justified. A seminary professor once told me, "Try to explain election, and you may lose your mind. But explain it away—and you may lose your soul!"

We will never understand the total concept of election this side of heaven. But we should not ignore this important doctrine that is taught throughout the Bible. Let's notice some obvious facts about divine election.

1. *Salvation begins with God.* "God hath from the beginning chosen you to salvation" (2 Thes. 2:13). "Ye have not chosen Me, but I have chosen you" (John 15:16). "He [the Father] hath chosen us in Him [Christ] before the foundation of the world" (Eph. 1:4). The entire plan of salvation was born in the heart of God long before man was created or the universe formed.

2. *Salvation involves God's love.* Paul called these saints "brethren beloved"—not only beloved by Paul (see 2:17), but also beloved by God. God's love made Calvary possible (Rom. 5:8), and there Jesus Christ died for our sins. But it is not only God's love that saves the sinner; it is God's grace. God in His grace gives us what we do not deserve, and God in His mercy does not give us what we do deserve. This explains why Paul often opened his letters with, "Grace be unto you, and peace, from God our Father, and the Lord Jesus Christ" (1:1).

3. *Salvation involves faith.* "For by grace are ye saved through faith" (Eph. 2:8). Paul, Silas (Silvanus is the Roman spelling), and Timothy brought

the Gospel to Thessalonica and preached in the power of God (1:5). Some people who heard the message believed and turned from their vain idols to the true and living God (1:9). The Spirit of God used the Word of God to generate faith (Rom. 10:17). Paul called this "sanctification of the Spirit and belief of the truth" (2 Thes. 2:13).

4. *Salvation involves the Trinity.* As you read this letter, you discover the doctrine of the Trinity. Christians believe in one God existing in three Persons: God the Father, and God the Son, and God the Holy Spirit. Keep in mind that all three Persons are involved in our salvation. This will help you escape dangerous extremes that either deny human responsibility or dilute divine sovereignty— for both are taught in the Bible.

As far as God the Father is concerned, I was saved when He chose me in Christ before the world began. As far as God the Son is concerned, I was saved when He died for me on the cross. As far as God the Holy Spirit is concerned, I was saved one Saturday night in May 1945, when I heard the Word and trusted Jesus Christ. At that moment, the entire plan fell together and I became a child of God. If you had asked me that night if I was one of the elect, I would have been speechless. At that time I knew nothing about election. But the Holy Spirit witnessed in my heart that I was a child of God.

5. *Salvation changes the life.* How did Paul know that these Thessalonians were elected of God? He saw a change in their lives. If you put 1:3 next to 1:9-10, you will get the picture:

your work of faith   you turned to God
                                      from idols

| your labor of love | to serve the living and true God |
| and patience of hope | to wait for His Son from heaven |

The person who claims to be one of God's elect, but whose life has not changed, is only fooling himself. *Those whom God chooses, He changes.* This does not mean they are perfect, but they are possessors of a new life that cannot be hidden.

Faith, hope, and love are the three cardinal virtues of the Christian life, and the three greatest evidences of salvation. *Faith* must always lead to works (James 2:14-26). It has been said, "We are not saved by faith plus works, but by a faith that works." If the Thessalonians had continued to worship their dead idols while professing faith in the living God, it would have proved that they were not among God's elect.

Love is also an evidence of salvation: "the love of God is shed abroad in our hearts by the Holy Ghost which is given unto us" (Rom. 5:5). We are "taught by God to love one another" (1 Thes. 4:9). We serve Christ because we love Him; this is the "labor of love" that Paul mentioned. "If ye love Me, keep My commandments" (John 14:15).

The third evidence of salvation is *hope,* waiting for Jesus Christ to return (1:10). The return of Jesus Christ is the dominant theme of both of these Thessalonian letters. Unsaved people are not eagerly awaiting the Lord's return. In fact, when our Lord catches His church up into the air, unsaved people will be totally surprised (5:1-11).

Faith, hope, and love are evidences of election. These spiritual qualities are bound together and can come only from God. For further evidence, see these passages: 1 Corinthians 13:13; Romans 5:2-5; Galatians 5:5-6; Colossians 1:4-5; Hebrews 6:10-12 and 10:22-24; 1 Peter 1:21-22.

A local church must be composed of elect people, those who have been saved by the grace of God. One problem today is the presence, in the church family, of unbelievers whose names may be on the church roll, but not written in the Lamb's Book of Life. Every church member should examine his heart to determine whether he has truly been born again and belongs to God's elect.

An Exemplary People (1:5-7)

From the very inception of this church, Paul looked to them with joy and gratitude as Christians worthy of the name. They were examples in several areas of their lives.

1. They received the Word (1:5). The Gospel came to them through the ministry of Paul and his associates. Many traveling preachers and philosophers in that day were only interested in making money off of ignorant people. But the Holy Spirit used the Word in great power, and the Thessalonians responded by receiving both the message and the messengers. In spite of the persecution in Philippi, Paul and Silas had been "bold . . . to speak . . . the Gospel" (2:2); and the people believed and were saved. They never lost that eagerness for the Word of God (2:13).

2. They followed their spiritual leaders (1:6a). The word "followers" is actually "imitators." These new believers not only accepted the message and the messengers, but they also imitated their lives. This led to severe persecution. It is important that young Christians respect spiritual leadership and learn from mature believers. Just as a newborn

baby needs a family, so a newborn Christian needs
the local church and the leaders there. "Obey them
that have the [spiritual] rule over you, and submit
yourselves: for they watch for your souls" (Heb.
13:17). It is not enough for us as mature believers
to *win* souls; we must also *watch for* souls and encourage new Christians to obey God's Word.

3. *They suffered for Christ (1:6b).* In turning
from idols to serve God, these believers angered
their friends and relatives, and this led to persecution. No doubt some of them lost their jobs because of their new faith. Just as the Jewish
unbelievers persecuted the believers in Judea, so
the Gentile unbelievers persecuted the Thessalonian believers (2:14-16). Faith is always tested,
and persecution is one of the tests (Matt. 13:21;
2 Tim. 3:12).

4. *They encouraged other churches (1:7).* Christians either encourage or discourage each other.
This principle applies also to churches. Paul used
the churches of Macedonia as a stimulus for the
Corinthian church to give to the missionary offering
(2 Cor. 8:1-8). Even though they were new believers, the Thessalonians set a good example that
encouraged the surrounding assemblies. Churches
must never compete with one another in a worldly
manner, but they can "provoke unto love and to
good works" (Heb. 10:24).

In every way, the church at Thessalonica was
exemplary. The secret was found in their faith,
hope, and love; for these are the spiritual moti-
vators of the Christian life.

An Enthusiastic People (1:8)

Their "work of faith and labor of love" expressed
itself in their sharing of the Gospel with others.

They were both "receivers" (the Word came to them, 1:5) and "transmitters" (the Word went out from them, 1:8). Each believer and each local church must receive and transmit God's Word.

The verb *sounded out* actually means "to sound as a trumpet." But the Thessalonians were not "tooting their own horns" as did the Pharisees (Matt. 6:1-4). They were trumpeting forth the Good News of salvation, and their message had a clear and certain sound to it (1 Cor. 14:8). Wherever Paul went, the people told him about the faith of the Thessalonian believers.

It is the responsibility and privilege of each local church to share the message of salvation with the lost world. At the end of each of the four Gospels and at the beginning of the Book of Acts, there are commissions for the churches to obey (Matt. 28:18-20; Mark 16:15-16; Luke 24:46-49; John 20:21; Acts 1:8). Many congregations are content to pay a staff to do the witnessing and soul-winning. But in New Testament churches, the entire congregation was involved in sharing the Good News (Acts 2:44-47 and 5:42).

A recent survey of church growth indicated that 70 to 80 percent of a church's growth is the result of friends witnessing to friends and relatives to relatives. While visitation evangelism and other methods of outreach help, the personal contact brings the harvest.

But election and evangelism go together. The person who says, "God will save those He wants to save and He doesn't need my help!" understands neither election nor evangelism. In the Bible, election always involves *responsibility*. God chose Israel and made them an elect nation so that they might witness to the Gentiles.

In the same way, God has chosen the church that we might be witnesses today. The fact that we are God's elect people does not excuse us from the task of evangelism. On the contrary, the doctrine of election is one of the greatest encouragements to evangelism.

Paul's experience at Corinth (Acts 18:1-11) was a perfect illustration of this truth. Corinth was a wicked city, and it was not easy to start a church there. The people were godless sinners (1 Cor. 6:9-11), but Paul preached the Word faithfully. When persecution arose from the Jewish unbelievers, Paul moved from the synagogue into the house of Justus. Then the Lord encouraged Paul: "Be not afraid, but speak, and hold not thy peace: for I am with thee, and no man shall set on thee to hurt thee: for I have much people in this city" (Acts 18:9-10). The fact that God had His elect in Corinth encouraged Paul to remain there for a year and a half.

If salvation were the work of man, we would have every right to be discouraged and quit. But salvation is the work of God, and He uses people to call out His elect. "He called you by our Gospel" (2 Thes. 2:14). The same God who ordains *the end* (the salvation of the lost) also ordains *the means* to the end (the preaching of the Gospel). There is no conflict between divine sovereignty and human responsibility, even though we cannot reconcile the two.

We need more churches today where the people are enthusiastic to share the message of salvation with others. As I write this, 2.4 billion people in our world have no visible witness of the Gospel in their midst, or no church body. In spite of the outreach of radio, television, and the printing press, we are losing ground in the work of reaching the lost. Are you an enthusiastic Christian? Is your church enthusiastic about witnessing?

An Expectant People (1:9-10)

Their *work of faith* made them an elect people, for they turned to God from their idols and trusted Jesus Christ. Their *labor of love* made them an exemplary and enthusiastic people as they lived the Word of God and shared the Gospel. Their *patience of hope* made them an expectant people, looking for their Saviour's return.

In these verses, Paul related the second coming of Christ to their salvation. Because they had trusted Christ, they looked for His return with joyful expectancy and knew that they would be delivered "from the wrath to come" (1:10). Paul repeated this truth in 5:9-10, and he amplified it again in 2 Thessalonians 1:5-10.

When they worshiped idols, the Thessalonians had no hope. But when they trusted "the living God," they had a living hope. (See 1 Peter 1:2-3.) Those of us who have been brought up in the Christian doctrine cannot understand the bondage of pagan idolatry. Before Paul came to them with the Gospel, these people were without hope and "without God in the world" (Eph. 2:12). Read Psalm 115 for a vivid description of what it is like to worship an idol.

Christians are "children of the living God" (Rom. 9:26). Their bodies are the "temples of the living God" (2 Cor. 6:16), indwelt by the "Spirit of the living God" (2 Cor. 3:3). The church is "the church of the living God" (1 Tim. 3:15); and for His church, God is preparing "the city of the living God" (Heb. 12:22). The living God has given us a living hope by raising His Son Jesus Christ from the dead.

Two aspects of the Lord's return must be distinguished. First, Jesus Christ will come in the air for His church (1 Thes. 4:13-18). This will usher in a period of tribulation on the earth (1 Thes. 5:1-3). At the close of this period, He will return to the earth with His church (2 Thes. 1:5-10; Rev. 19:11-21), defeat His enemies, and then set up His kingdom (Rev. 20:1-6).

The word translated "wait" in 1:10 means "to await someone with patience and confidence, expectantly." Waiting involves activity and endurance. Some of the Thessalonian believers quit their work and became idle busybodies, arguing that the Lord was coming soon. But if we really believe the Lord is coming, we will prove our faith by keeping busy and obeying His Word. Our Lord's parable of the pounds (Luke 19:11-27) teaches that we must "occupy" (be busy; in this case, invest the money) till He returns.

Christians are waiting for Jesus Christ, and He may return at any time. We are not waiting for any "signs;" we are waiting for the Saviour. We are waiting for the redemption of the body (Rom. 8:23-25) and the hope of righteousness (Gal. 5:5). When Jesus Christ returns we shall receive new bodies (Phil. 3:20-21), and we shall be like Him (1 John 3:1-2). He will take us to the home He has prepared (John 14:1-6), and He will reward us for the service we have given in His name (Rom. 14:10-12).

A local church that truly lives in the expectation of seeing Jesus Christ at any time will be a vibrant and victorious group of people. Expecting the Lord's return is a great motivation for soul-winning

(2:19-20) and Christian stability (3:11-13). It is a wonderful comfort in sorrow (4:13-18) and a great encouragement for godly living (5:23-24). It is tragic when churches forget this wonderful doctrine. It is even more tragic when churches believe it and preach it—but do not practice it.

Paul remembered how this church was born (1:3), and he gave thanks for their spiritual characteristics: they were elect, exemplary, enthusiastic, and expectant. But churches are made up of individuals. When you and I speak of the church, we must never say "they." We should say "we." *We are the church!* This means that if you and I have these spiritual characteristics, our churches will become what God wants them to become. The result will be the winning of the lost and the glorifying of the Lord.

What every church should be is what every Christian should be: *elect* (born again), *exemplary* (imitating the right people), *enthusiastic* (sharing the Gospel with others), and *expectant* (daily looking for Jesus Christ to return).

Perhaps it is time for an inventory.

[1]For yourselves, brethren, know our entrance in unto you, that it was not in vain: [2]But even after that we had suffered and were shamefully entreated, as ye know, at Philippi, we were bold in our God to speak unto you the Gospel of God with much contention. [3]For our exhortation was not of deceit, nor of uncleanness, nor in guile: [4]but as we were allowed of God to be put in trust with the Gospel, even so we speak; not as pleasing men, but God, which trieth our hearts. [5]For neither at any time used we flattering words, as ye know, nor a cloke of covetousness; God is witness: [6]nor of men sought we glory, neither of you, nor yet of others, when we might have been burdensome, as the apostles of Christ. [7]But we were gentle among you, even as a nurse cherisheth her children: [8]so being affectionately desirous of you, we were willing to have imparted unto you, not the Gospel of God only, but also our own souls, because ye were dear unto us. [9]For ye remember, brethren, our labor and travail: for laboring night and day, because we would not be chargeable unto any of you, we preached unto you the Gospel of God.

[10]Ye are witnesses, and God also, how holily and justly and unblameably we behaved ourselves among you that believe: [11]as ye know how we exhorted and comforted and charged every one of you, as a father doth his children, [12]that ye would walk worthy of God, who hath called you unto His kingdom and glory.

1 Thessalonians 2:1-12

3

Helping the Baby Grow Up

Chapter 1 of 1 Thessalonians introduced us to Paul
the evangelist. This chapter introduces us to Paul
the pastor, for it explains how the great Apostle
cared for the new believers in the churches that he
founded. Paul considered "the care of all the
churches" (2 Cor. 11:28) a greater burden than
all the sufferings and difficulties he experienced in
his ministry (2 Cor. 11:23ff).

Just as God uses people to bring the Gospel to
the lost, so He uses people to nurture the babes
in Christ and help lead them to maturity. The
church at Thessalonica was born through the faithful *preaching* of the Apostle and his helpers, and
the church was nurtured through the faithful
pastoring that Paul and his friends gave to the infant church. This helped them stand strong in the
midst of persecution.

In these verses, Paul reminded them of the kind
of ministry he had as he taught and cared for the
young church. Three pictures of his ministry
emerge.

The Faithful Steward (2:1-6)

Paul had been "put in trust with the Gospel" (2:4). It was not a message that he made up or that he received from men (Gal. 1:11-12). Paul looked on himself as a steward of God's message.

A steward owns nothing, but possesses and uses everything that belongs to his master. Joseph was a steward in the household of Potiphar (Gen. 39:1-6). He managed his master's affairs and used all his master's goods to promote his master's welfare. Every steward one day must give an account of his stewardship (Luke 16:1-2). If he is found unfaithful, he will suffer.

The message of the Gospel is a treasure God has entrusted to us. We must not bury it; we must invest it so it will multiply and produce "spiritual dividends" to God's glory. Some Christians think that the church's only responsibility is to protect the Gospel from those who would change it (Gal. 1:6-9). But we also must *share* the Gospel; otherwise, we are protecting it in vain.

Faithfulness is the most important quality a steward possesses (1 Cor. 4:1-2). He may not be popular in the eyes of men; but he dare not be unfaithful in the eyes of God. "Not as pleasing men, but God who trieth [testeth] our hearts" (2:4). The Christian who "plays to the grandstands" will lose God's approval. When we see the characteristics of Paul's ministry as a steward, we understand what faithfulness means.

1. The manner of his ministry (2:1-2). Paul and Silas had been beaten and humiliated at Philippi; yet they came to Thessalonica and preached. Most of us would have taken a vacation or found an excuse not to minister. Paul was courageous—he was not a quitter. He had a "holy boldness" that was born of dedication to God. Like the other apostles before him, Paul boldly proclaimed the Good News (Acts 4:13, 29, 31).

His preaching was "with much contention." This is an athletic term that means "a contest, a struggle." The Greek world was familiar with athletic contests, and Paul often used this idea to illustrate spiritual truths (1 Cor. 9:24-27; Phil. 3:13-14; 2 Tim. 4:7). He used this same word in Philippians 1:30 where he pictured the Christian life as an athletic contest that demanded dedication and energy. It had not been easy to start a church in Philippi, and it was not easy to start one in Thessalonica.

2. The message of his ministry (2:3a). "For the appeal we make does not spring from error" (NIV). Here he assured them that his message was true. Six times in this letter he mentioned the Gospel. This message of Christ's death and resurrection (1 Cor. 15:1-6) is a true message and is the only true Gospel (Gal. 1:6-12). Paul received this Gospel from God, not from man. It is the only Good News that saves the lost sinner.

3. The motive of his ministry (2:3b). He was not guilty of "uncleanness," for his motives were pure. It is possible to preach the right message with the wrong motives (Phil. 1:14-19). Unfortunately, some people in Paul's day used religion as a means for making money. Paul did not use the Gospel as "a cloak to cover his covetousness" (2:5). He was open and honest in all his dealings, and he even worked at a trade to earn his own support. (See 2 Thes. 3:8-10.)

Paul was very sensitive about money matters. He did not want to give anyone a reason to accuse him of being a religious salesman (1 Cor. 9:1-18).

As an apostle, he had the privilege of receiving support. But he gave up that right in order to be free from any possible blame that would disgrace the ministry.

4. *The method of his ministry (2:3c).* Paul did not use guile or trickery to win converts. The word translated "guile" carries the idea of "baiting a hook." In other words, Paul did not trap people into being saved, the way a clever salesman traps people into buying his product. Spiritual witnessing and "Christian salesmanship" are different. Salvation does not lie at the end of a clever argument or a subtle presentation. It is the result of God's Word and the power of the Holy Spirit (1:5).

Often we hear, "I don't care what your method is, just so long as your message is right." But some methods are unworthy of the Gospel. They are cheap, whereas the Gospel is a costly message that required the death of God's only Son. They are worldly and man-centered, whereas the Gospel is a divine message centered in God's glory.

Paul's enemies in Thessalonica accused him of being a cheap peddler of this new message. They said that his only motive was to make money. In describing himself as a faithful steward, Paul answered these critics; *and Paul's readers knew that he told the truth.* (Trace that phrase "as ye know" in 1:5; 2:1, 5, 11; 3:3-4; 4:2; 5:2.) Paul appealed to the witness of God (2:5) and to their own witness. He had "a conscience void of offense toward God, and toward men" (Acts 24:16).

Paul abhorred flattery (2:5). David also hated this sin. "They speak vanity everyone with his neighbor; with flattering lips and with a double heart do they speak" (Ps. 12:2).

I once read that a flatterer is a person who

manipulates rather than communicates. A flatterer can use either truth or lies to achieve his unholy purpose, which is to control your decisions for his own profit.

Some people even flatter themselves. "For he flatters himself in his own eyes" (Ps. 36:2, RSV). This was the sin of Haman, that evil man in the Book of Esther. He was so interested in flattering himself that he even plotted to slaughter all the Jews to achieve that goal.

Some people try to flatter God. "Nevertheless they [Israel] did flatter Him [God] with their mouth, and they lied unto Him with their tongues" (Ps. 78:36). Flattery is another form of lying. It means saying one thing to God with our lips while our hearts are far from Him (Mark 7:6).

Some Christians try to win friends and influence people by appealing to their egos. A true ministry of the Gospel deals honestly (but lovingly) with sin and judgment and leaves the unbeliever with nothing to boast of in himself. Paul's method was as pure as his motive: he presented the Word of God in the power of the Spirit, and trusted God to work.

The Loving Mother (2:7-8)
The emphasis of the steward is *faithfulness;* the emphasis of the mother is *gentleness.* As an apostle, Paul was a man of authority; but he always used his authority in love. The babes in Christ sensed his tender loving care as he nurtured them. He was indeed like a loving mother who cared for her children.

It takes time and energy to care for children. Paul did not turn his converts over to baby-sitters; he made sacrifices and cared for them himself. He

did not tell them to "read a book" as a substitute
for his own personal ministry (though good Christian literature can help young believers to grow).

Paul had patience with the new Christians. Our
four children are into adulthood now, but I can
assure you that my wife and I needed a great deal
of patience before they reached that state. (To
even things up, our parents needed patience with
us!) Children do not grow up instantly. They all
experience growing pains and encounter problems
as they mature. Paul's love for them made him
patient, because love suffers long, and is kind
(1 Cor. 13:4).

Paul also nourished them. Verse 7 can read "even
as a nursing mother cherishes her own children."
What is the lesson here? *A nursing mother imparts
her own life to the child.* This is exactly what Paul
wrote in verse 8. You cannot be a nursing mother
and turn your baby over to someone else. That
baby must be in your arms, next to your heart.

The nursing mother eats the food and transforms
it into milk for the baby. The mature Christian
feeds on the Word of God and then shares its
nourishment with the younger believers so they can
grow (1 Peter 2:1-3). A nursing child can become
ill through reaction to something the mother has
eaten. The Christian who is feeding others must be
careful not to feed on the wrong things himself.

Besides making sacrifices, having patience, and
giving nourishment, a mother also *protects* her
child. It was this fact that enabled King Solomon
to discover which woman was the real mother of
the living child (1 Kings 3:16-28). Paul was willing
to give not only the Gospel but his own life as well.
His love for the Thessalonians was so great he
would die for them if necessary.

But it is not easy to be a "nursing mother." Even Moses felt the burden of caring for God's people. "Was it I who conceived all this people? Was it I who brought them forth, that Thou shouldest say to me, 'Carry them in your bosom as a nurse carries a nursing infant, to the land which Thou didst swear to their fathers'?" (Num. 11:12, NASB) But if we do not nurse the new Christians on the milk of the Word, they can never mature to appreciate the meat of the Word (Heb. 5:10-14).

The Concerned Father (2:9-12)

Paul considered himself a "spiritual father" to the believers at Thessalonica, just as he did toward the saints at Corinth. "For if you were to have countless tutors in Christ, yet you would not have many fathers; for in Christ Jesus I became your father through the Gospel" (1 Cor. 4:15, NASB). The Spirit of God used the Word of God in Paul's ministry, and many people in Thessalonica were born again into the family of God.

But the father not only begets the children; he also cares for them. As he defended his own work against false accusations, Paul pointed out three of his duties as the spiritual father to the Thessalonicans.

1. His work (2:9). The father works to support his family. Even though the Christians in Philippi sent financial help (Phil. 4:15-16), Paul still made tents and paid his own way. No one could accuse him of using his ministry for his own profit. Later on, Paul used this fact to shame the lazy Christians in the Thessalonican church (2 Thes. 3:6ff.).

Paul used the words "labor and travail." J. B. Phillips translated these words "our struggles and hard work." "Toil and hardship" would be another translation. It was not easy to make tents and minister the Word at the same time. No wonder Paul toiled "night and day" (Acts 20:31). He toiled because he loved the believers and wanted to help them as much as possible. "For I seek not yours, but you: for the children ought not to lay up for the parents, but the parents for the children" (2 Cor. 12:14).

2. *His walk (2:10).* Fathers must live so that they are good examples to their children. He could call the Thessalonican believers as witnesses that his life had been exemplary in every way. None of the members of the assembly could accuse Paul of being a poor example. Furthermore, *God* had witnessed Paul's life; and Paul was not afraid to call God as a witness that he had lived a dedicated life, while caring for the church family.

His life was holy. In the Greek, this means to "carefully fulfill the duties God gives to a person." Our word *pious* is close to it, if you think of piety at its best and not as some fake kind of religion. This same word is applied to the character of God in Revelation 15:4 and 16:5.

His life was also righteous. This refers to integrity, uprightness of character and behavior. This is not the "righteousness of the law" but the practical righteousness that God works out in our lives as we yield to Him (Phil. 3:4-10).

Paul's life was also unblamable. Literally, this word means "not able to find fault in." His enemies might accuse him, but no one could level any charge against Paul and prove it. Christians are supposed to be "blameless and harmless" as they live in this world (Phil. 2:15).

3. *His words (2:11-12).* A father must not only support the family by working, and teach the

family by being a good example. He must also take time to speak to the family members. Paul knew the importance of teaching these new believers the truths that would help them grow in the Lord.

Paul dealt with each of the believers *personally.* "For you know that we dealt with each of you as a father deals with his own children" (2:11, NIV). As busy as he was, Paul still had time for personal counseling with the members of the assembly. While it is good for church leaders to address the larger group, spending time with people on a one-to-one basis is also needed. Our Lord was never too busy to speak to individuals, even though He preached to great multitudes. To be sure, this is difficult and demanding work. But it is rewarding work that glorifies God.

Paul *encouraged* the new believers. This is what a father does with his children, for children are easily discouraged. New Christians need someone to encourage them in the Lord. The word "exhorting" in our Authorized Version means "to call to one's side, to encourage." It does not mean that Paul scolded them. Rather, it means he encouraged them to go on with the Lord.

I once received a letter from a radio listener who thanked me for the encouragement of the messages she had heard. "When we go to church," she wrote, "all our pastor does is scold us and whip us. We really get tired of this. It's refreshing to hear some words of encouragement!"

Paul also *comforted* them. This word carries the same idea of "encouragement," with the emphasis on *activity.* Paul not only made them feel better, but he made them want to *do* better. A father must not pamper a child; rather, he must encourage the child to go right back and try over again. Christian

encouragement must not become an anesthetic that
puts us to sleep. It must be a stimulant that awak-
ens us to do better.

Finally, Paul *charged* them. This word means
that Paul "testified to them" out of his own experience with the Lord. It carries the idea of giving
personal witness. Sometimes we go through difficulties so that we may share with new Christians
what the Lord has done. God "comforts us in all
our troubles, so that we can comfort those in any
trouble with the comfort we ourselves have received from God" (2 Cor. 1:4, NIV).

We who are parents know that our children
(especially teenagers) do not like to hear us say,
"Now, back when I was a kid . . ." But this is an
important part of training a family. It is a wonderful thing when a "spiritual father" can encourage
and help his "children" out of his own experience
with the Lord. "Come, ye children, hearken unto
me: I will teach you the fear of the Lord" (Ps.
34:11).

What was the purpose for this fatherly ministry
to the believers? His aim was that his children
might "walk worthy of God" (2:12). Just as a
father wants to be proud of his children, so the
Lord wants to get glory through the lives of His
children. "I was very glad to find some of your
children walking in truth" (2 John 4, NASB). Paul
ministered to them in such a personal way because
he was teaching them how to walk.

Every child must learn how to walk. He must
have good models to follow. Paul admonished them
to walk "worthy of the Lord." (See Col. 1:10 and
Phil. 1:27.) We are to walk worthy of the calling
we have in Christ Jesus (Eph. 4:1). God has called
us; we are saved by grace. We are a part of His

kingdom and glory. One day we shall enter the eternal kingdom and share His glory. This assurance ought to govern our lives and make us want to please the Lord.

The verb in verse 12 is in the present tense: "who is continually calling you." God called us to salvation (2 Thes. 2:13-14), and He is constantly calling us to a life of holiness and obedience. "But as He which hath called you is holy, so be ye holy in all manner of conversation [behavior]; because is is written, 'Be ye holy, for I am holy'" (1 Peter 1:15-16).

This passage gives us a beautiful example of New Testament follow-up. Paul has shown us how to raise the babies. We must be faithful stewards, loving mothers, and concerned fathers. If we are not faithful to God, we may find ourselves becoming doting mothers and pampering fathers. Children need discipline as well as love. In fact, discipline is one evidence of love.

No wonder the church at Thessalonica prospered in spite of persecution, and shared the Gospel with others for miles around. They had been born right (chapter 1) and nurtured right (chapter 2). This is a good example for us to follow.

[13]For this cause also thank we God without ceasing, because, when ye received the Word of God which ye heard of us, ye received it not as the word of men, but as it is in truth, the Word of God, which effectually worketh also in you that believe. [14]For ye, brethren, became followers of the churches of God which in Judea are in Christ Jesus: for ye also have suffered like things of your own countrymen, even as they have of the Jews: [15]who both killed the Lord Jesus, and their own prophets, and have persecuted us; and they please not God, and are contrary to all men: [16]forbidding us to speak to the Gentiles that they might be saved, to fill up their sins alway: for the wrath is come upon them to the uttermost.

[17]But we, brethren, being taken from you for a short time in presence, not in heart, endeavoured the more abundantly to see your face with the great desire. [18]Wherefore we would have come unto you, even I Paul, once and again; but Satan hindered us.

[19]For what is our hope, or joy, or crown of rejoicing? Are not even ye in the presence of our Lord Jesus Christ at His coming? [20]For ye are our glory and joy.

1 Thessalonians 2:13-20

4

Growing Pains

It was not easy to be a Christian in Thessalonica where believers faced persecution and suffering. Their situation explains Paul's choice of words: *affliction* (1:6; 3:3), which means "pressure from circumstances"; *suffered* (2:14), the same word used for our Lord's sufferings; *persecuted* (2:15), meaning "driven out and rejected"; *contrary* (2:15), used of winds that blow against and hinder progress; and *hindered* (2:18), which pictures a road so broken that travel is blocked.

Yet in the midst of suffering, the Thessalonian Christians experienced joy. They received Paul's ministry of the Word "in much affliction, with joy of the Holy Spirit" (1:6). Paul certainly was burdened for his brethren who were going through suffering, and yet he also had joy (2:19-20). It was a fulfillment of our Lord's promise, "In the world ye shall have tribulation: but be of good cheer; I have overcome the world" (John 16:33).

Churches do experience "growing pains" as they seek to win the lost and glorify the Lord. We may not experience the same kind of political and religious persecution that the early Christians suffered (though in some parts of the world today the persecution is just as intense as it was then). Yet if we are living "godly in Christ Jesus," we will suffer for His sake (2 Tim. 3:12). In this paragraph, Paul explained the divine resources we have in times of suffering and persecution.

God's Word within Us (2:13)

The church has been founded on the Word of God (1:6), the message of the Gospel of Jesus Christ. The same Word that brings us salvation also enables us to live for Christ and endure suffering for His sake. Paul was thankful that the saints in Thessalonica had the right spiritual attitudes toward the Word of God. This helped them endure in the hour of suffering.

1. They appreciated the Word. They did not receive it as the word of men; they received it as the Word of God. We must never treat the Bible as any other book, for the Bible is different in origin, character, content, and cost. The Bible is the Word of God. It was inspired by the Spirit of God (2 Tim. 3:16) and written by men of God who were used by the Spirit (2 Peter 1:20-21). God's Word is holy, pure, and perfect (Ps. 19:7-9). The Bible was written at great cost, not only to the writers, but to Jesus Christ who became Man that the Word of God might be given to us.

The way a Christian treats his Bible shows how he regards Jesus Christ. He is the living Word (John 1:1, 14), and the Bible is the written Word; but *in essence* they are the same. Both are bread (John 6:48; Matt. 4:4), light (John 8:12; Ps. 119:105), and truth (John 14:6; 17:17). The Holy

Spirit gave birth to Jesus Christ through a holy woman (Luke 1:35), and He gave birth to the Bible through holy men of God (2 Peter 1:20-21). Jesus Christ is the eternal Son of God forever (Rom. 1:25), and the Word of God will live forever (Ps. 119:89; 1 Peter 1:23, 25).

It may be a personal prejudice, but I dislike seeing a Bible on the floor or at the bottom of a stack of books. If I am carrying several books with my Bible, I try to remember to put the Bible on the top. If we appreciate the Bible as the inspired Word of God, then we will reveal this appreciation in our treatment of the Bible.

Would you rather have your Bible than *food?* Job said, "I have esteemed the words of His mouth more than my necessary food" (Job 23:12). God's Word is *bread* (Matt. 4:4), *milk* and *meat* (Heb. 5:11-14), and even *honey* (Ps. 119:103). Mary chose the Word, but her sister Martha got involved in making a meal (Luke 10:38-42). Mary got the blessing while Martha lost the victory.

Would you rather have God's Word than *money?* The believer who wrote Psalm 119 made it clear that God's Word meant more to him than "all riches" (v. 14), "thousands of gold and silver" (v. 72), "fine gold" (v. 127), and even "great spoil" (v. 162).

I recall a young couple I sought to help in one of my churches. They had a lovely little son, but they were very careless about attending church and Sunday School. The little boy was not getting the Christian training he needed. A visit to the home told me why: the father wanted more money and so he worked on Sundays to make double time. He did not *have* to work on the Lord's Day, but he wanted the money rather than God's Word. He earned more money, but he was never able to keep it. The little son became ill and the extra money went to doctors.

Would you rather have God's Word than *sleep?* "My eyes anticipate the night watches, that I may meditate on Thy Word" (Ps. 119:148, NASB). The Jews had three night watches: sunset to 10, 10 to 2, and 2 until dawn. The psalmist gave up sleep three times each night that he might spend time with the Word. But some Christians cannot get out of bed on Sunday morning to study the Word.

If we are going to be victorious in suffering, we must appreciate the Word. But there is a second attitude we must show toward the Bible.

2. They appropriated the Word. Paul used two different words for "received": the first means simply "to accept from another," while the second means "to welcome." One means "the hearing of the ear" while the other means "the hearing of the heart." The believers at Thessalonica did not only *hear* the Word; they took it into their inner man and made it a part of their lives.

The Lord Jesus repeatedly warned people about the wrong kind of hearing, and His warnings are still needed. "Who hath ears to hear, let him hear" (Matt. 13:9). In other words, "Take heed *that* you hear." Use every opportunity you have to hear the Word of God.

But He gave another warning in Mark 4:24: "Take heed *what* ye hear." How often believers hear the Word of God in Sunday School and church, and then get in their cars, turn on the radio, and listen to programs that help erase the impressions made by the Word. When we visited church congregations in Great Britain, my wife and I were impressed with their practice of sitting down after the benediction. They meditated on the Word and allowed the Spirit to minister to them. This is far better than rushing out of church and joking with friends.

Our Lord's third warning is in Luke 8:18: "Take heed therefore *how* ye hear." Many people are careless hearers and cannot apply themselves to listen to the teaching of God's Word. These people have "itching ears" and want religious entertainment (2 Tim. 4:3). Some of them are "dull of hearing" (Heb. 5:11), too lazy to apply themselves and pay attention. One of these days our churches will be hungry because of a famine "for hearing the words of the Lord" (Amos 8:11). Too many churches have substituted entertainment for the preaching of God's Word, and many people no longer welcome the Word of God.

How do we appropriate the Word? By understanding it and receiving it into our hearts, and by meditating on it so that it becomes part of the inner man. Meditation is to the spiritual life what digestion is to the physical life. If you did not digest your food, you would die. It takes time to meditate, but it is the only way to appropriate the Word and grow.

3. They applied the Word. They obeyed the Word by faith, and the Word went to work in their lives. It is not enough to appreciate the Bible, or even to appropriate the Bible. We must apply the Word in our lives and be hearers and doers of the Word (James 1:19-25).

The Word of God has in it the power to accomplish the will of God. "For nothing is impossible with God" (Luke 1:37, NIV). It has well been said, "God's commandments are God's enablements." Jesus commanded the crippled man to stretch out

his hand—the very thing the man could not do.
Yet that Word of command gave him the power to
obey. He trusted the Word, obeyed, and was made
whole (Mark 3:1-5). When we believe God's Word
and obey, He releases power—divine energy—that
works in our lives to fulfill His purposes.

The Word of God within us is a great source of
power in times of testing and suffering. If we appreciate the Word (the heart), appropriate the
Word (the mind), and apply the Word (the will),
then the whole person will be controlled by God's
Word and He will give us the victory.

God's People around Us (2:14-16)

In my pastoral work, I often found that suffering
people can become very self-centered and think
that they are the only ones going through the
furnace. Everyone goes through the normal human
suffering such as sickness, pain, and bereavement.
But I am referring to the suffering we endure *because we are Christians.*

Perhaps your family has disowned you because
of your faith; or perhaps you have been bypassed
for a promotion at work because you are a Christian. These experiences hurt, but they are not ours
alone. Other Christians are going through the same
trials, and many, in other parts of the world, face
much greater difficulty.

Not only were the Thessalonian saints imitators
of the Lord and of Paul (1:6), but they also became imitators of the Jewish believers in their
experience of persecution. The saints in Judea suffered at the hands of the Jews, and the saints in
Thessalonica suffered at the hands of the Gentiles.
But keep in mind that even this Gentile persecution was encouraged by the Jewish unbelievers

(Acts 17:5, 13). Jesus promised that this would happen (John 15:18-27).

Was Paul giving evidence of "religious bigotry" when he accused the Jews of killing Jesus Christ and persecuting the Christians? No, he was simply stating a fact of history. Nowhere does the Bible accuse *all* Jews of what *a few Jews* did in Jerusalem and Judea when Christ was crucified and the church founded. The Romans also participated in the trial and death of Christ, and, for that matter, it was *our sins* that sent Him to the cross (Isa. 53:6). There is no place in the Christian faith for anti-Semitism. Paul himself loved his fellow Jews and sought to help them (Acts 24:17; Rom. 9:1-5).

God called Israel to be a blessing to all the world (Gen. 12:1-3 and 22:18). Through Israel He gave the promises and the covenants, and the Word of God; and through Israel, Jesus Christ the Saviour came into the world. "Salvation is of the Jews" (John 4:22). The first Christians were Jews, as was Paul, the greatest Christian missionary.

Why, then, did the leaders of Israel officially reject Jesus Christ and persecute His followers? *They were only repeating the sins of their fathers.* Their ancestors had persecuted the prophets long before Jesus came to earth (Matt. 5:10-12). They could not see that their Law was only a temporary preparation for God's New Covenant of grace. By rejecting God's truth, they protected their man-made traditions (Mark 7:1-8). Our Lord's parable in Luke 20:9-19 explained their sinful attitudes.

The sad thing was that Israel was filling up their sins (2:16) and storing up wrath for the day of judgment. This image is used in Genesis 15:16, and Jesus used it in His sermon against the Pharisees (Matt. 23:32). God patiently waits as sinners rebel against Him, and He watches as their measure of sin and judgment fills up. When the time is up, God's patience will end and judgment will fall.

In one sense, judgment had already fallen on Israel; for they were a scattered people, and their nation in Palestine was under Roman rule. (See Deut. 28:15ff.) But an even greater judgment was to fall in the future; for in A.D. 70 the Roman armies besieged Jerusalem, destroyed the city and the temple, and ended the period of God's patience with His people during the ministry of the apostles (see Matt. 22:1-11). It is tragic but true that the righteous suffered because of the sins of the wicked:

Paul encouraged the suffering Christians by assuring them that their experiences were not new or isolated. Others had suffered before them and were even then suffering with them. The churches in Judea had not been exterminated by suffering; if anything, they had been purified and increased. But the persecutors were filling up the measure of wrath to be heaped on their heads. Saints have been saved to the uttermost (Heb. 7:25), but sinners will experience wrath to the uttermost (2:16).

Here is one of the great values of the local church: we stand together in times of difficulty and encourage one another. It was when Elijah isolated himself from the other faithful Israelites that he became discouraged and wanted to quit. One reason Paul sent Timothy back to Thessalonica was to encourage the believers (1 Thes. 3:1-4). A lonely saint is very vulnerable to the attacks of Satan. We need each other in the battles of life.

God's Glory before Us (2:17-20)

Paul was not ashamed to state his affection for the Thessalonian Christians. He felt as though he had been "orphaned" from them (2:17) since he was their spiritual mother and father (2:7, 11). Paul wanted to remain there longer to help ground them in the faith, but the enemy drove him out. However, his absence was only physical; he was still with them in heart (see Phil. 1:7).

Paul made every effort possible to return to them, though Satan was "breaking up the road and putting up obstacles" (literal meaning of "hindered" in 2:18). Paul had the same kind of deep desire to be with them as Jesus had to be with His disciples before His death (Luke 22:15).

But Paul did not look back and give in to regret and remorse. Instead, he looked ahead and rejoiced. For the Christian, the best is yet to come. Paul looked ahead by faith and saw his friends in the presence of Jesus Christ in glory.

In times of trouble and testing, it is important that we take the long view of things. Paul lived in the future tense, as well as in the present. His actions were governed by what God would do in the future. He knew that Jesus Christ would return and reward him for his faithful ministry; and on that day, the saints from Thessalonica would bring glory to God and joy to Paul's heart. As the familiar song says, "It will be worth it all, when we see Jesus."

The fact that we shall one day stand at the Judgment Seat of Christ ought to motivate us to be faithful in spite of difficulties. We must remember that *faithfulness* is the important thing (1 Cor. 4:2). At the Judgment Seat of Christ, our works will be judged and rewards will be given (1 Cor. 4:1-5; 2 Cor. 5:9-10; Rom. 14:10-12). In his letters, Paul often pictured these rewards as *crowns*. The word used signified the "victor's crown" at the races, not the royal crown of the king. It is the word *stephanos* from which we get the names Stephen and Stephanie.

Paul did not say that he would receive a crown, though this is suggested. He said that *the saints themselves* would be his crown when he met them at the Judgment Seat. To be sure, some of the believers in the church were not living as they should, and some were a burden to Paul. But when he looked ahead and saw them in glory, they brought joy to his heart.

This joy of greeting believers in heaven also brings with it a solemn warning: we will lose joy if we go to heaven empty-handed. The Christian who has not sincerely tried to win others to Christ will not experience this glory and joy when Jesus Christ returns. It is not enough to "wait for His Son" (1:10). We must also witness for God and work for His Son, so that when we get to heaven, we will have trophies to present for His glory. There is a special joy and reward for the soul-winner (Dan. 12:3).

There is also a crown for the believer who subdues his body and keeps it controlled for the glory of God (1 Cor. 9:24-27). Self-control is produced by the Spirit (Gal. 5:23). Since our bodies are God's temples, we must be careful not to defile them. The ultimate in giving the body to God is dying for His sake; and for this there is a crown (Rev. 2:10). Those who lovingly look for Christ's appearing will receive the "crown of righteousness" (2 Tim. 4:8). The faithful pastor can anticipate the "crown of glory" (1 Peter 5:4).

We must never look on future rewards as a means of showing up the other saints. Like the elders described in Revelation 4:4 (a picture of the glorified church), we will worship the Lord and lay our crowns at His feet (Rev. 4:10). After all, our work was done in His power and for His glory, so He deserves all the praise.

The fact that God promises rewards to us is another evidence of His grace. God could demand our service simply on the basis of all He has done for us. Our motive for serving Him is love. In His grace, He gives us rewards so that we may have something to give Him in return.

When the Christians at Thessalonica read this letter, it must have encouraged them tremendously. They were going through intense persecution and suffering, and perhaps some of them were tempted to give up.

"Don't give up!" Paul encouraged them. "Lay hold of the spiritual resources you have in Jesus Christ. You have the Word of God within you, the people of God around you, and the glory of God before you. There is no need to give up."

¹Wherefore when we could no longer forbear, we thought it good to be left at Athens alone; ²and sent Timotheus our brother, and minister of God, and our fellowlaborer in the Gospel of Christ, to establish you, and to comfort you concerning your faith: ³that no man should be moved by these afflictions: for yourselves know that we are appointed thereunto. ⁴For verily, when we were with you, we told you before that we should suffer tribulation; even as it came to pass, and ye know. ⁵For this cause, when I could no longer forbear, I sent to know your faith, lest by some means the tempter have tempted you, and our labor be in vain. ⁶But now when Timotheus came from you unto us, and brought us good tidings of your faith and charity, and that ye have good remembrance of us always, desiring greatly to see us, as we also to see you: ⁷therefore, brethren, we were comforted over you in all our affliction and distress by your faith: ⁸for now we live, if ye stand fast in the Lord. ⁹For what thanks can we render to God again for you, for all the joy wherewith we joy for your sakes before our God; ¹⁰night and day praying exceedingly that we might see your face, and might perfect that which is lacking in your faith? ¹¹Now God Himself and our Father, and our Lord Jesus Christ, direct our way unto you. ¹²And the Lord make you to increase and abound in love one toward another, and toward all men, even as we do toward you: ¹³to the end He may stablish your hearts unblamable in holiness before God, even our Father, at the coming of our Lord Jesus Christ with all His saints.

1 Thessalonians 3:1-13

5

Take a Stand!

Before a child can walk, he must learn to stand. Usually the father and mother teach the child to stand and then to walk. Paul was "spiritual parent" to these believers, but he had been forced to leave Thessalonica. How, then, could he help these young Christians learn to stand in the trials of life?

In the first two chapters, Paul explained how the church was born and nurtured. Now he dealt with the next step in maturity: how the church was to stand. The key word in this chapter is *establish* (3:2, 13). The key thought is expressed in verse 8: "For now we live, if ye stand fast in the Lord."

Paul explained three ministries that he performed to help these new Christians become firmly established.

He Sent Them a Helper (3:1-5)

When Paul and his friends left Thessalonica, they went to Berea and ministered the Word. But the troublemakers from Thessalonica followed them and stirred up opposition. Paul left for Athens while Silas and Timothy remained at Berea. (See Acts 17:10-15.) Apparently, Timothy did join Paul in Athens (note the "we" in 1 Thes. 3:1-2), but Paul sent him back to Thessalonica to help the young church that was going through tribulations. Several important factors were involved in this move.

1. Paul's concern (3:1). The "wherefore" that opens this chapter refers to 2:17-20, where Paul expressed his great love for the believers. It was because of this love that he could not abandon them when they needed spiritual help. Paul was not only an evangelist; he was also a pastor. He knew that soul-winning was but one part of the commission God gave him. These new believers must also be taught and established in the faith.

Instead, Paul chose to be left alone in Athens so that Timothy could return to Thessalonica and establish the saints. The word translated "left" in verse 1 means "to leave loved ones at death." In 1 Thessalonians 2:17 he said that he felt "orphaned" from his friends in Thessalonica, and the Greek word can also mean "bereaved." Paul was not a "hireling shepherd" who abandoned the sheep when there was danger (John 10:12-13). To leave these new believers was like an experience of death.

This is a good lesson for Christian workers today. Paul so loved the Thessalonican believers that he would have risked his own life to return to them. He so loved the saints at Philippi that he was willing to stay out of heaven in order to encourage them (Phil. 1:22-26). He wanted to give of himself and his resources for them, as a parent provides for loved children. "I will very gladly spend and be spent for you" (2 Cor. 12:15).

2. Timothy's character (3:2). Not every believer is equipped to establish other Christians in the faith. Ideally, every Christian should be mature enough to help other Christians grow in the Lord and learn to stand on their own two feet. Unfortunately, some Christians are like those described in Hebrews 5:11-14. They have gone backward in their spiritual walk and have forgotten the basic truths of the Word. Instead of teaching others, they themselves need to be taught again. They are going through a second childhood spiritually.

Timothy was the ideal man to send to the church to help them stand firm. Timothy and Titus were Paul's "special agents" whom he used as troubleshooters whenever the churches had problems. Paul sent Timothy to Corinth to help straighten out the problems there (1 Cor. 16:10-11). He also planned to send Timothy to help the saints in Philippi (Phil. 2:19-23).

What kind of a person can help younger believers grow in the Lord? To begin with, *he must be a Christian himself:* "Timothy, our brother. . ." (3:2). We cannot lead another where we have not been ourselves, nor can we share that which we do not possess. Paul had led Timothy to faith in Christ (1 Tim. 1:2) so that he was truly a brother.

But Timothy was also *a minister.* This is simply the Greek word for a servant. Our English word *deacon* comes from this word, *diakonos.* Timothy was not afraid to work. He had faithfully served with Paul (Phil. 2:22) and knew how to minister in the churches. It is a demanding thing to establish new Christians. They have many problems and often do not grow as fast as we think they should. Teaching them requires love and patience, and Timothy had these qualities.

Timothy was a good *team man;* he was a "fellow worker." He did not try to run the show himself and get people to follow him. To begin with, he was a fellow worker with God. It was God who worked in and through Timothy to accomplish His work. (See Phil. 2:13 and 1 Cor. 3:9.)

But Timothy was also a fellow worker with the other believers. He obeyed Paul and left Athens for Thessalonica. He returned to Paul in Corinth with news about the Thessalonican church. No wonder Paul wrote of him: "For I have no man like-minded, who will naturally care for your state" (Phil. 2:20).

3. *The church's conflict (3:3-5).* The trials and testings that come to our lives as Christians are not accidents—they are *appointments.* We must expect to "suffer for His sake" (Phil. 1:29). Persecution is not foreign to the believer (1 Peter 4:12ff.), but a normal part of the Christian life. Paul had repeatedly told them this while he was with them. We must warn new believers that the way is not easy as they seek to live for Christ; otherwise, when trials come, these babes in Christ will be discouraged and defeated.

Of course, behind these persecutions is Satan, the enemy of the Christian (3:5). He is the tempter, and he seeks to ruin our faith. Note the emphasis on *faith* in this chapter (vv. 5, 6, 7, 10). As a roaring lion, Satan stalks believers; and we must resist him "stedfast in the faith" (1 Peter 5:8-9). When Satan tempted Eve, he began by weakening her faith in God: "Yea, hath God said . . . ?" (Gen. 3:1) As a serpent, Satan deceives (2 Cor. 11:3); as a lion, he devours (1 Peter 5:8). He will use any means to attack the Christian and weaken his faith in God.

The word "moved" in verse 3 is interesting. It literally means "to wag the tail, to fawn over." The idea is that Satan often flatters the believer in order to lead him astray. Satan told Eve she would be like God if she ate of the tree, and she fell for his flattery. Satan is more dangerous when he flatters than when he frowns.

Timothy's task was to establish these believers and encourage (comfort) them in their faith. It is faith in God that keeps our feet on the ground when the enemy attacks. Without faith in God, we are defeated. "This is the victory that overcometh the world, even our faith" (1 John 5:4).

He Wrote a Letter (3:6-8)

Timothy met Paul at Corinth (Acts 18:5) and gave him the glad news that things were going well at Thessalonica. The phrase "brought us good tidings" is the exact equivalent of "preaching the good news of the Gospel." The report from Timothy was, to Paul, like hearing the Gospel.

Timothy reported that the new believers were standing firm in spite of persecution. They did not believe the lies that the enemy had told about Paul, but they still held him in the highest esteem in love.

Paul's response was to write them this letter. Paul wrote some letters which are not a part of the New Testament (1 Cor. 5:9), but the two letters to the Thessalonican church are a part of God's inspired Word.

This suggests that God's Word is one of the best tools for establishing new Christians in the faith. "So then, brothers, stand firm and hold to the teachings we passed on to you, whether by word of mouth or by letter" (2 Thes. 2:15, NIV). When

Jesus was tempted by Satan, He used the Word of
God to defeat him (Matt. 4:1-11). Paul admonished
the Ephesian believers to take "the sword of the
Spirit, which is the Word of God" (Eph. 6:17) in
their battle against Satan and his demonic as-
sistants.

The Bible is able to establish us because it is
inspired of God (2 Tim. 3:16). It is not simply a
book of religious ideas or good moral advice; it is
the very Word of God. It is "profitable for doctrine,
for reproof, for correction, for instruction in righteousness." It has well been said that *doctrine* tells
us what is right, *reproof* tells us what is not right,
correction tells us how to get right, and *instruction*
tells us how to stay right.

First Thessalonians is saturated with Bible doctrines. Every major doctrine of the faith is touched
on in these brief chapters. There are dozens of
references to God the Father and Jesus Christ, and
at least four references to the Holy Spirit (1:5-6;
4:8; 5:19). In this epistle, Paul dealt with sin and
salvation, the doctrine of the church, the work of
the ministry, and especially the doctrine of the last
things. Since Paul did not remain in Thessalonica
very long, it is remarkable that he taught his converts so much.

Dr. R. W. Dale was pastor of Carr's Lane Con-
gregational Church in England for nearly 50 years.
He began a series of sermons on basic Bible doctrine, knowing that his members could not stand
firm in their faith if they did not know what they
believed or why they believed it. A fellow pastor
said to Dr. Dale, "They will never take it." But
Dale replied, "They will *have to* take it!" And they
did, to the strengthening of the church.

When I became a Christian, churches did not

have regular follow-up courses for new converts such as we have today. My "follow-up course" was a series of Bible studies from the Book of Hebrews, led by a gifted layman and taught in his living room. Much of what was taught was over my head as a new believer. But what I did learn grounded me in the Word and established me in the faith.

A working knowledge of the Bible is essential for spiritual growth and stability. God's Word is *food* to nourish us (Matt. 4:4), *light* to guide us (Ps. 119:105), and a *weapon* to defend us (Eph. 6:17). "Thus saith the Lord!" is our sure foundation. One reason God has established local churches is that believers might grow in the Word and, in turn, help others to grow (2 Tim. 2:2; Eph. 4:11-16).

Paul sent them a man, and that man established them in the Word. Paul ministered to them in a third way.

He Prayed for Them (3:9-13)

The Word of God and prayer should go together. The prophet Samuel told the people of Israel, "God forbid that I should sin against the Lord in ceasing to pray for you: but I will teach you the good and the right way" (1 Sam. 12:23). Peter said, "But we [the apostles] will give ourselves continually to prayer, and to the ministry of the Word" (Acts 6:4). Paul had this same emphasis: "And now, brethren, I commend you to God [prayer], and to the Word of His grace, which is able to build you up" (Acts 20:32).

Jesus prayed for His disciples, just as Paul prayed for the Thessalonican Christians, that their faith would not fail (Luke 22:31-32). I ministered for several weeks in Kenya and Zaire, and when I arrived home, I was more convinced than ever that the greatest need of missionaries and national churches is *prayer*. We must also pray for young Christians here at home. It is not enough to teach them Bible truth; we must also support them in our prayers.

Paul prayed for three specific requests. First, he prayed *that their faith might mature* (3:10). Paul asked God to make it possible for him to minister to them personally, but God did not answer that request. Paul longed to see them again; he longed to minister to them and help bring their faith to maturity. The word translated "perfect" has the meaning of "adjust, equip, furnish." It is even used for the mending of nets (Mark 1:19). Our faith never reaches perfection; there is always need for adjustment and growth. We go "from faith to faith" (Rom. 1:17).

Abraham is a good illustration of this principle. God called him to the land of Canaan, and when he arrived, he discovered a famine. God permitted that famine so that Abraham's faith might be tested. Unfortunately, Abraham failed the test and went down to Egypt for help.

Each step of the way, God brought circumstances to bear on Abraham that forced him to trust God and grow in his faith. Faith is like a muscle: it gets stronger with use. Abraham had problems with his worldly nephew, Lot. He also had problems with his wife and her handmaid, Hagar. The ultimate test of faith came when God asked Abraham to sacrifice his beloved son, Isaac.

Faith that cannot be tested cannot be trusted. God tries our faith, not to destroy it, but to develop it. Had Abraham not learned to trust God in the famine, he could never have trusted Him in the other difficulties. Paul prayed that the suffering Christians in Thessalonica might grow in their faith, and God answered his prayer. Paul wrote in his second letter, "We are bound to thank God always for you, brethren . . . because that your faith groweth exceedingly" (2 Thes. 1:3).

Paul's second request was *that their love might abound* (3:12). Times of suffering can be times of selfishness. Persecuted people often become very self-centered and demanding. What life does to us depends on what life finds in us; and nothing reveals the true inner man like the furnace of affliction. Some people build walls in times of trial, and shut themselves off. Others build bridges and draw closer to the Lord and His people. This was Paul's prayer for these believers, and God answered it: "the charity of every one of you all toward each other aboundeth" (2 Thes. 1:3).

Our growing faith in God ought to result in a growing love for others. We are "taught of God to love one another" (1 Thes. 4:9), and some of these lessons are best learned in the school of suffering. Joseph suffered for 13 years because of his brothers' envy and persecution. Yet he learned to love them in spite of their hatred. The Jewish legalists persecuted Paul from city to city, yet Paul so loved his people that he willingly would have died for them (Rom. 9:1-3).

When I counsel young couples in preparation for marriage, I often ask the man: "If your wife became paralyzed three weeks after you were married, do you love her enough to stay with her and care for her?" True love deepens in times of difficulty; shallow romance disappears when difficulties appear.

But true Christian love is shown not only to

believers, but also "toward all men" (3:12). We love one another, but we also love the lost and our enemies. Abounding love must not be bound. It must be free to expand and touch all men.

Paul's third request was for *holiness of life* (3:13). Again, it is the return of Jesus Christ that motivates the believer to live a holy life. Our Lord's return is also a source of stability in the Christian life. Where there is stability, there can be sanctity; and where there is holiness, there is assurance. The two go together.

Notice that Paul's prayers for his friends were not careless or occasional. He prayed "night and day"; he prayed "exceedingly," which is the same word translated "exceeding abundantly" in Ephesians 3:20. True prayer is hard work. Epaphras must have learned from Paul how to pray for people: "always laboring fervently . . . that ye may stand perfect and complete in all the will of God" (Col. 4:12).

The entire Trinity is involved in this prayer. Paul addressed the Father and Son in verse 11. In verse 12 "the Lord" may refer to the Holy Spirit, since "our Lord" at the end of verse 13 certainly refers to Jesus Christ. If this is so, then this is the only prayer I know of in the New Testament directed to the Holy Spirit. The Bible pattern of prayer is: to the Father, through the Son, and in the Spirit. Since the Holy Spirit is the Sanctifier of the believer, and this is a prayer for holy living, the address is proper.

Paul ended chapter 2 with a reference to the place of the saints at the return of Christ, and he ended this chapter in the same way. He prayed that his converts might stand blameless and holy before God at Christ's return. Since all believers will be transformed to be like Christ when He returns (1 John 3:2), Paul could not be referring to our personal condition in heaven. He was referring to our lives here on earth as they will be reviewed at the Judgment Seat of Christ. We will never face our sins in heaven, for they are remembered against us no more (Rom. 8:1; Heb. 10:14-18). But our works will be tested, and you cannot separate conduct from character.

Paul's prayer teaches us how to pray not only for new believers, but for *all* believers. We should pray that their faith will mature, their love grow, and their character and conduct be holy and blameless before God. "And every man that hath this hope in Him [Christ] purifieth himself, even as He is pure" (1 John 3:3).

As we review this chapter, we see how important it is to care for new Christians. Leading someone to Christ is not enough. We must also lead him on in the Christian life and help him get established. If he is not established, he will fall when the winds of persecution start to blow. If he cannot stand, he will never learn to walk.

What shall we do? We can be an encouragement and stand at his side as he matures. We can share the Word of God. We can pray. This is what Paul did—and it worked.

[1]Furthermore then we beseech you, brethren, and exhort you by the Lord Jesus, that as ye have received of us how ye ought to walk and to please God, so ye would abound more and more. [2]For ye know what commandments we gave you by the Lord Jesus. [3]For this is the will of God, even your sanctification, that ye should abstain from fornication: [4]that every one of you should know how to possess his vessel in sanctification and honor; [5]not in the lust of concupiscence, even as the Gentiles which know not God: [6]that no man go beyond and defraud his brother in any matter: because that the Lord is the Avenger of all such, as we also have forewarned you and testified. [7]For God hath not called us unto uncleanness, but unto holiness. [8]He therefore that despiseth, despiseth not man, but God, who hath also given unto us His Holy Spirit. [9]But as touching brotherly love ye need not that I write unto you: for ye yourselves are taught of God to love one another. [10]And indeed ye do it toward all the brethren which are in Macedonia: but we beseech you, brethren, that ye increase more and more; [11]and that ye study to be quiet, and to do your own business, and to work with your own hands, as we commanded you; [12]that ye may walk honestly toward them that are without, and that ye may have lack of nothing.

1 Thessalonians 4:1-12

6

How to Please
Your Father

Along with jogging, walking has become a popular exercise and outdoor sport. As I drive in the city of Chicago, I often see individuals and entire families enjoying a walk in the park or in the forest preserves. When driving on the highway, I sometimes wave to "walking parties" heading for some distant rendezvous.

The Christian life can be compared to a walk. In fact, this is one of Paul's favorite pictures: "Walk worthy of the vocation wherewith ye are called" (Eph. 4:1); "walk not as other Gentiles walk" (Eph. 4:17); "walk in love" (Eph. 5:2); "walk as children of light" (Eph. 5:8).

The Christian life begins with a step of faith. But that step leads to a walk of faith, "For we walk by faith, not by sight" (2 Cor. 5:7). Walking suggests progress, and we must make progress in the Christian life (Heb. 6:1; Phil. 3:13-16). Walking also demands strength, and God has promised, "As thy days, so shall thy strength be" (Deut. 33:25).

But we must be sure to "walk in the light" for

the enemy has put traps and detours to catch us
(1 John 1:5-7). Of course, at the end of life's walk,
we will step into the very presence of the Lord.
"And Enoch walked with God, and he was not, for
God took him" (Gen. 5:24).

Paul described a threefold walk for the Christian
to follow.

Walk in Holiness (4:1-8)

The moral climate in the Roman Empire was not
healthy. Immorality was a way of life; and, thanks
to slavery, people had the leisure time to indulge
in the latest pleasures. The Christian message of
holy living was new to that culture, and it was not
easy for these young believers to fight the temptations around them. Paul gave four reasons why
they should live a holy life and abstain from
sensual lusts.

1. To please God (4:1). Everybody lives to please
somebody. Many people live to please themselves.
They have no sensitivity to the needs of others.
"The soul of a journey," wrote William Hazlitt, "is
liberty, perfect liberty, to think, feel, do just as one
pleases." That advice may work for a vacation, but
it could never work in the everyday affairs of life.
Christians cannot go through life pleasing only
themselves (Rom. 15:1).

We must also be careful when it comes to pleasing others. It is possible to both please others and
honor God, but it is also possible to dishonor God.
"For if I yet pleased men, I should not be the
servant of Christ" (Gal. 1:10). This had been Paul's
attitude when he ministered in Thessalonica. "Even
so we speak, not as pleasing men but God, who
trieth our hearts" (1 Thes. 2:4).

Pleasing God ought to be the major motive of

the Christian life. Children should live to please their father. The Holy Spirit works in our lives "both to will and to do of His good pleasure" (Phil. 2:13). Enoch walked with God, and before God called him to heaven, Enoch "had this testimony, that he pleased God" (Heb. 11:5). Jesus said, "I do always those things that please Him" (John 8:29).

Pleasing God means much more than simply doing God's will. It is possible to obey God and yet not please Him. Jonah is a case in point. He obeyed God and did what he was commanded, but his heart was not in it. God blessed His Word but He could not bless His servant. So Jonah sat outside the city of Nineveh angry with everybody, including the Lord! Our obedience should be "not with eyeservice, as men-pleasers, but as the servants of Christ, doing the will of God from the heart" (Eph. 6:6).

How do we know what pleases God? How do we know what pleases an earthly father? By listening to him and living with him. As we read the Word, and as we fellowship in worship and service, we get to know the heart of God; and this opens us up to the will of God.

2. *To obey God (4:2-3)*. When he ministered in Thessalonica, Paul gave the believers the commandments of God regarding personal purity. The word *commandments* is a military term. It refers to orders handed down from superior officers. We are soldiers in God's army, and we must obey orders. "No one serving as a soldier gets involved in civilian affairs—he wants to please his commanding officer" (2 Tim. 2:4, NIV).

In verse 3, Paul reminded these new believers that sexual immorality did not please God. God created sex, and He has the authority to govern its use. From the beginning, He established marriage as a sacred union between one man and one woman. God created sex both for the continuance of the race and for the pleasure of the marriage partners. "Marriage should be honored by all, and the marriage bed kept pure" (Heb. 13:4, NIV). God's commandments concerning sex are not for the purpose of robbing people of joy, but rather of protecting them that they might not lose their joy. "Thou shalt not commit adultery" builds a wall around marriage that makes the relationship not a prison, but a safe and beautiful garden.

We never have to seek to know the will of God in this matter; He has told us clearly. "Abstain from fornication" is His commandment, and no amount of liberal theology or modern philosophy can alter it. Throughout the Bible, God warns against sexual sin; and these warnings must be heeded. God's purpose is *our sanctification,* that we might live separated lives in purity of mind and body.

3. To glorify God (4:4-5). This is the positive side of God's commandment. Christians are supposed to be different from the unsaved. The Gentiles (unsaved) do not know God; therefore, they live ungodly lives. But we know God, and we are obligated to glorify Him in this world. "God's plan is to make you holy, and that entails first of all a clean break with sexual immorality" (1 Thes. 4:3, PH).

"Possess his vessel" in verse 4 probably means "control his body," for our bodies are the vessels of God (see 2 Cor. 4:7 and 2 Tim. 2:20-21). But it can also mean "learn to live with his own wife," for the wife is called "the weaker vessel" (1 Peter

3:7). I prefer the first interpretation, for Paul wrote to *all* Christians, not just the married ones. The Christian who commits sexual sin is sinning against his own body (1 Cor. 6:19-20), and he is robbing God of the glory He should receive through a believer's way of life.

This explains why God gives such demanding requirements for spiritual leadership in the church (1 Tim. 3). If spiritual leaders cannot rule in their own homes, how can they lead the church? If we glorify God in our bodies, then we can glorify Him in the body which is the church.

4. To escape the judgment of God (4:6-8). God is no respecter of persons; He must deal with His children when they sin (Col. 3:23-25). A church member criticized her pastor because he was preaching against sin in the lives of Christians. "After all," she said, "sin in the life of a believer is different from sin in the lives of unsaved people." "Yes," replied the pastor, "*it is worse.*"

While it is true that the Christian is not under condemnation (John 5:24 and Rom. 8:1), it is also true that he is not free from the harvest of sorrow that comes when we sow to the flesh (Gal. 6:7-8). When King David committed adultery, he tried to cover his sin, but God chastened him severely. (Read Psalms 32 and 51 to see what he lost during those months.) When David confessed his sins, God forgave him; *but God could not change the consequences.* David reaped what he sowed, and it was a painful experience for him.

"But I am one of God's elect!" a Christian may argue. "I belong to Him, and He can never cast me out." Election is not an excuse for sin—it is an encouragement for holiness. "For God hath not called us unto uncleanness, but unto holiness"

(4:7). "But as He which hath called you is holy, so be ye holy" (1 Peter 1:15). The privilege of election also involves responsibilities of obedience (Deut. 7:6, 11).

A holy walk involves a right relationship with God the Father (who called us), God the Son (who died for us), and God the Spirit (who lives within us). It is the presence of the Holy Spirit that makes our body the temple of God (1 Cor. 6:19-20). Furthermore, it is by walking in the Spirit that we get victory over the lusts of the flesh (Gal. 5:16ff). To despise God's commandments is to invite the judgment of God and also to grieve the Spirit of God.

How does the Spirit of God help us live a clean life, free from sexual impurity? To begin with, He creates holy desires within us so that we have an appetite for God's pure Word (1 Peter 2:1-3) and not the polluted garbage of the flesh (Rom. 13:12-14). Also, He teaches us the Word and helps us to recall God's promises in times of temptation (John 14:26; Eph. 6:17). As we yield to the Spirit, He empowers us to walk in holiness and not be detoured into the lusts of the world and the flesh. The fruit of the Spirit overcomes the works of the flesh (Gal. 5:16-26).

Paul devoted a great deal of space to this theme of sexual purity because it was a critical problem in the church of that day. *It is also a critical problem in the church today.* For many people, marriage vows are no longer considered sacred, and divorce (even among believers) is no longer governed by the Word of God. There are "gay churches" where homosexuals and lesbians "love one another" and claim to be Christians. Premarital sex and "Christian pornography" are accepted parts

of the religious landscape in many places. Yet God
has said, "Walk in holiness."

Walk in Harmony (4:9-10)

The transition from *holiness* to *love* is not a difficult one. Paul made this transition in his prayer
recorded in 1 Thessalonians 3:11-13. Just as God's
love is a holy love, so our love for God and for one
another ought to motivate us to holy living. The
more we live like God, the more we will love one
another. If a Christian really loves his brother, he
will not sin against him (1 Thes. 4:6).

There are four basic words for "love" in the
Greek language. *Eros* refers to physical love; it
gives us our English word *erotic*. Eros love does
not have to be sinful, but in Paul's day its main
emphasis was sensual. This word is never used in
the New Testament. Another word, *storge* (pro-
nounced STOR-gay), refers to *family love,* the love
of parents for their children. This word is also
absent from our New Testament, although a related word is translated "kindly affectioned" in
Romans 12:10.

The two words most used for love are *philia*
(fil-E-uh) and *agape* (a-GA-pay). *Philia* love is
the love of deep affection, such as in friendship
or even marriage. But *agape* love is the love God
shows toward us. It is not simply a love based on
feeling; it is expressed in our wills. Agape love
treats others as God would treat them, regardless
of feelings or personal preferences.

The word *philadelphias* is translated "brotherly
love." Because Christians belong to the same
family, and have the same Father, they should love
one another. In fact, we are "taught of God to
love one another." God the Father taught us to

love each other when He gave Christ to die for us on the cross. "We love, because He first loved us" (1 John 4:19, NIV). God the Son taught us to love one another when He said, "A new commandment I give unto you, that ye love one another" (John 13:34). And the Holy Spirit taught us to love one another when He poured out the love of God in our hearts (Rom. 5:5) when we trusted Christ.

Have you noticed that animals do *instinctively* what is necessary to keep them alive and safe? Fish do not attend classes to learn how to swim (even though they swim in schools), and birds by nature put out their wings and flap them in order to fly. It is *nature* that determines action. Because a fish has a fish's nature, it swims; because a hawk has a hawk's nature, it flies. And because a Christian has God's nature (2 Peter 1:4), he loves, because "God is love" (1 John 4:8).

Faith, hope, and love had been the distinctive characteristics of the Thessalonican Christians from the beginning (1 Thes. 1:3). Timothy had reported the good news of their love (1 Thes. 3:6), so Paul was not exhorting them to acquire something they did not already possess. He was encouraging them to get more of what they already enjoyed. You can never have too much Christian love. Paul had prayed that their love might "increase and abound" (1 Thes. 3:12); and God answered that prayer (see 2 Thes. 1:3).

How does God cause our love to "increase more and more"? By putting us into circumstances that force us to practice Christian love. Love is the "circulatory system" of the body of Christ, but if our spiritual muscles are not exercised, the circulation is impaired. The difficulties that we believers have *with one another* are opportunities for us to

grow in our love. This explains why Christians who
have had the most problems with each other often
end up loving one another deeply, much to the
amazement of the world.

Walk in Honesty (4:11-12)

The word in verse 12 that is translated "honestly"
in our Authorized Version, carries the meaning of
"becomingly, in a seemly way." It is translated
"decently" in 1 Corinthians 14:40, "Let all things
be done decently and in order." The emphasis is
on the believer's witness to those who are outside
the Christian fellowship. "Them that are without"
is a familiar description of unbelievers.

Christians not only have the obligation to love
one another but also to be good testimonies to the
people of the world. Paul's great concern was that
the Thessalonican believers earn their own wages
and not become freeloaders depending on the support of unbelievers. "Make it your ambition to lead
a quiet life" (v. 11, NIV) seems like a paradox; if
you are ambitious, your life will probably not be
quiet. But the emphasis is on quietness of mind
and heart, the inner peace that enables a man to be
sufficient through faith in Christ. Paul did not want
the saints running around creating problems as
they earned their daily bread.

For the most part, the Greeks despised manual
labor. Most of the work was done by slaves. Paul,
of course, was a tentmaker; and he was careful in
Thessalonica to set the example of hard work. (See
1 Thes. 2:6 and 2 Thes. 3:6ff.) Unfortunately, some
of the new believers in the church misunderstood
the doctrine of Christ's return and gave up their
jobs in order to wait for His coming. This meant
that they were supported by other Christians, some

of whom may not have had sufficient funds for their own families. It also meant that these fanatical people could not pay their bills, and therefore they lost their testimony with the unsaved merchants.

"My wife is going to have plastic surgery," a man said to his friend. "I'm taking away all of her credit cards!" How easy it is to purchase things we do not need with money we do not have, and then lose not only our credit, but also our good Christian witness. "If therefore you have not been faithful in the use of unrighteous mammon [money] who will entrust the true riches to you?" (Luke 16:11, NASB) Churches and Christians who defend their orthodoxy but do not pay their bills have no orthodoxy to defend.

"Mind your own business and work with your hands" (v. 11, NIV) was what Paul commanded them. Idle people spend their time interfering with the affairs of others and getting themselves and others into trouble. "We hear that some among you are idle. They are not busy; they are busybodies" (2 Thes. 3:11, NIV). "But let none of you suffer . . . as a busybody in other men's matters" (1 Peter 4:15).

Believers who are about the Father's business (Luke 2:49) do not have the time—or desire—to meddle in the affairs of others. Unfortunately, even a Bible class could become an opportunity for gossip ("so that you might pray more intelligently") and a substitute for true Christian service.

As believers, we must be careful in our relationships with "those that are without." It requires spiritual grace and wisdom to have contact without contamination and to be different without being judgmental and proud. "Walk in wisdom toward them that are without" (Col. 4:5). If we lack this spiritual wisdom, we will do more harm than good.

There are several good reasons why Christians should work, not the least of which is to provide for their own families (1 Tim. 5:8). If unsaved people have to work to pay their bills, why should Christians be exempt? We also work in order to be able to give to those who have need (Eph. 4:28); but "if any would not work, neither should he eat" (2 Thes. 3:10). Work is not a curse; it is a blessing. God gave Adam work to do in Paradise. It is the toil and sweat of work that belongs to the curse, and not the work itself (Gen. 2:15 and 3:17ff.).

As we review this section, we see how practical the Christian walk really is. The obedient Christian will have *a holy life* by abstaining from sexual sin; *a harmonious life,* by loving the brethren; and *an honest life,* by working with his hands and not meddling in the affairs of others. When unsaved people see Christ magnified in this kind of a life, they will either oppose it with envy or desire to have it for themselves. Either way, God is glorified.

[13]But I would not have you to be ignorant,' brethren, concerning them which are asleep, that ye sorrow not, even as others which have no hope. [14]For if we believe that Jesus died and rose again, even so them also which sleep in Jesus will God bring with Him. [15]For this we say unto you by the Word of the Lord, that we which are alive and remain unto the coming of the Lord shall not prevent them which are asleep. [16]For the Lord Himself shall descend from heaven with a shout, with the voice of the archangel, and with the trump of God: and the dead in Christ shall rise first; [17]then we which are alive and remain shall be caught up together with them in the clouds, to meet the Lord in the air: and so shall we ever be with the Lord. [18]Wherefore comfort one another with these words.

1 Thessalonians 4:13-18

7

The Comfort of His Coming

The pagan world in Paul's day had no hope of life after death. A typical inscription on a grave demonstrates this fact:

> I was not
> I became
> I am not
> I care not

While some of the philosophers, such as Socrates, sought to prove happiness after death, the pagan world had no word of assurance.

The believers in Thessalonica were concerned about their loved ones who had died. What if the Lord should return? Would their deceased loved ones be handicapped in any way? Will those who are alive at His coming have an advantage over the believers who have died? In this paragraph, Paul answered their questions. He based his encouragement and comfort on five fundamental facts.

Revelation: We Have God's Truth (4:13, 15a)

How can mortal man penetrate beyond the grave and find assurance and peace for his own heart? From Old Testament days till the present, mankind has tried to solve the riddle of death and the afterlife. Philosophers have wrestled with the question of immortality. Spiritists have tried to communicate with those who have gone beyond.

In our modern world, scientists have investigated the experiences of people who claimed to have died and returned to life again. They have also studied occult phenomena, hoping to find a clue to the mystery of life after death.

Paul solved the problem when he wrote, "For this we say unto you by the Word of the Lord" (4:15). We Christians need not wonder about death or life after death, for we have a revelation from God in His Word. Why substitute human speculation for divine revelation?

It is important to note that the revelation concerning death and the afterlife was not given all at one time. Many cults use verses from the Psalms and Ecclesiastes to "prove" their false doctrines. These verses seem to teach that the grave is the end, or that the soul "sleeps" till the resurrection. We must keep in mind that God's revelation was *gradual* and *progressive,* and that it climaxed in the coming of Christ "who abolished death, and brought life and immortality to light through the Gospel" (2 Tim. 1:10, NASB). We look to Christ and the New Testament for the complete revelation concerning death.

God gave Paul a special revelation concerning the resurrection and the return of Christ (see 1 Cor. 15:51-54). What Paul taught agreed with what

Jesus taught (John 5:24-29 and 11:21-27). And God's revelation is based on the historic fact of Christ's resurrection. Since our Saviour has conquered death, we need not fear death or the future (1 Cor. 15:12ff). The authority of God's Word gives us the assurance and comfort we need.

Return: Christ Is Coming Again (4:14-15)

We have noted the emphasis on the return of Christ in the Thessalonian letters. Paul related Christ's return to salvation (1:9-10), service (2:19-20), and stability (3:11-13). In this paragraph, he related it to sorrow, and he showed how the doctrine of Christ's return can comfort the brokenhearted.

Paul applied the word *sleep* to those believers who died. Jesus used the same expression (John 11:11-13). Paul was careful to state that Jesus *died;* the word *sleep* is not applied to His experience. It is because He died that we need not fear death.

However, Paul did not say that the soul went to sleep at death. He made it clear that the soul of the believer went to be with the Lord: "them also which sleep in Jesus will God bring with Him" (v. 14). He cannot bring them when He returns unless they are with Him. It is not the soul that sleeps; *it is the body.* The Bible definition of death is given in James 2:26—"For as the body without the spirit is dead . . .". At death, the spirit leaves the body, and the body goes to sleep and no longer functions. The soul-spirit goes to be with the Lord, if the person has trusted Jesus Christ. "Absent from the body, and . . . present with the Lord" (2 Cor. 5:8).

The fact of our Lord's return is comfort to us

in bereavement, because we know that He will bring with Him His people who have "died in the Lord." I recall stating to a friend, "I hear you lost your wife. I'm very sorry." He replied, "No, I didn't lose her. You can't lose something when you know where it is—*and I know where she is!*" On the authority of the Word of God, we also know what will happen: Jesus Christ will one day return and bring His people with Him.

When will this event occur? Nobody knows, and it is wrong to set dates. The fact that Paul used the pronoun *we* in verses 15 and 17 suggests that he expected to be alive when the Lord returned. Theologians call this the doctrine of the imminent return of Christ. *Imminent* means that it can happen at any moment. As Christians, we do not look for signs, nor must any special events transpire before the Lord can return. These great events will take place "in a moment, in the twinkling of an eye" (1 Cor. 15:52).

Jesus Christ will return *in the air*, and this is where we shall meet Him (v. 17). Suddenly, millions of people will vanish! One summer our church camp staff staged an elaborate "rapture" while the camp director was off the grounds. When he returned, everybody was missing, clothing was on the ground as though people had "passed through" it, a motorboat was circling on the lake without pilot or passengers, and everything in the kitchen was functioning without a cook. A carefully timed phone call from town, ("Hey, what's happening? Everybody's missing over here!") only added to the effect. "I've got to admit," said the director, "it really shook me for a minute." Just think of what effect this event will have on a lost world!

Whether we Christians live or die, we have nothing to fear because Jesus will come either *with us* or *for us!* The fact of His return is a comfort to our hearts.

Resurrection: The Christian Dead Will Rise (4:15-16)

When Paul preached the doctrine of the resurrection to the Athenian philosophers, most of them mocked him (Acts 17:32). To the Greeks, *being rid of the body* was their great hope. Why would any man want to have his body resurrected? Furthermore, *how* could his body be resurrected, when the elements of the body would decay and become a part of the earth? To them, the doctrine of resurrection was foolish and impossible.

When Jesus Christ returns in the air, He will issue the "shout of command" and the "dead in Christ shall rise first" (4:16). This does not mean that He will put the elements of the body together again, for resurrection is not "reconstruction." Paul argued for the resurrection in 1 Corinthians 15:35ff. He pointed out that the resurrection of the human body is like the growing of a plant from a seed. The flower is not the identical seed that was planted, yet there is continuity from seed to plant. Christians shall receive glorified bodies, like the glorified body of Christ (Phil. 3:20-21; 1 Cor. 15:47-58). The dead body is the "seed" that is planted in the ground; the resurrection body is the "flower" that comes from that seed.

Passages like John 5:28-29 and Revelation 20:1-6 indicate that there are *two* resurrections in the future. When Jesus Christ returns in the air, He will call to Himself only those who are saved through faith in Him. This is called "the first resurrection" or "the resurrection of life." At the end of time, just before God ushers in the new heaven and earth, there will be another resurrection. This is called "the second resurrection" or "the resurrection of judgment." Between these two events, I believe that the Tribulation on earth and the 1000-year-kingdom will occur.

In Paul's day, the Pharisees believed in the resurrection of the dead, but the Sadducees did not (Acts 23:8). Jesus taught the doctrine of the resurrection and silenced the Sadducees (Matt. 22:23-33). The Old Testament Scriptures taught this doctrine (Job 14:13-15, and 19:23-27; Ps. 16:9-11; Dan. 12:2). The fact that Jesus arose from the dead proves that there is a resurrection.

Three unique sounds will be involved in this event: the Lord's shout, the sound of the trumpet, and the voice of the archangel. Jesus Christ will give "a shout of command," just as He did outside the tomb of Lazarus (John 11:43). Those "in the graves shall hear His voice" (John 5:28).

First Corinthians 15:52 also relates His return to the sound of a trumpet. The Jewish people were familiar with trumpets, because trumpets were used to declare war, to announce special times and seasons, and to gather the people for a journey (see Num. 10). In the Roman Empire, trumpets were used to announce the arrival of a great person. When God gave the Law to Israel, the event was preceded by a trumpet blast (Ex. 19:18-20).

Why "the voice of the archangel"? The only archangel who is named in the Bible is Michael (Jude 9), who apparently has a special ministry to Israel (Dan. 10:21 and Rev. 12:7). According to Daniel 10:13, there is more than one archangel; so we cannot be sure that it will be Michael's voice. At any rate, the angelic hosts will share in the victory shout when Jesus Christ comes.

The Christian doctrine of resurrection assures us that death is not the end. The grave is not the end. The body goes to sleep, but the soul goes to be with the Lord (Phil. 1:20-24). When the Lord returns, He will bring the soul with Him, will raise the body in glory, and will unite body and soul into one being to share His glory forever. This leads us to the fourth fact that gives us comfort and assurance in the face of death.

Rapture: Living Believers Caught Up (4:17)

The word *rapture* is not used in this section, but that is the literal meaning of "caught up." The Latin word *rapto* means "to seize, to carry off;" and from it we get our English word "rapture."

I once heard the Greek scholar, Dr. Kenneth S. Wuest, preach on this passage and explain the various meanings of the Greek word that is translated "caught up" in verse 17. Each of these meanings adds a special truth to the doctrine of our Lord's return.

"To catch away speedily." This is the translation in Acts 8:39, where the Spirit "caught away Philip" after he had led the Ethiopian to Christ. When the Lord returns in the air, we who are alive will be caught away quickly, in the twinkling of an eye. This means we should live each moment in the expectation of our Lord's return, lest He come and find us out of His will (1 John 3:1-3).

"To seize by force." See John 6:15. Does this suggest that Satan and his armies will try to keep us from leaving the earth? I trust it does not suggest that some of the saints will be so attached to

the world that they must literally be dragged away. Like Lot being delivered from Sodom, they will be scarcely saved (Gen. 19:16).

"To claim for one's own self." This views the Rapture from our Lord's point of view as He comes to claim His Bride.

"To move to a new place." Paul used this word when he described his visit to heaven (2 Cor. 12:1-4). Jesus Christ has gone to prepare a home for us (John 14:1-6), and when He comes, He will take us to that glorious place. We are pilgrims and strangers in this world. Our true citizenship is in heaven (Phil. 3:20-21).

"To rescue from danger." See Acts 23:10. This suggests that the church will be taken home *before* the time of Tribulation that will come to the world from God. First Thessalonians 1:10 and 5:9 seem to state this clearly.

Will the unsaved world be aware of what is happening? Will they hear the shout, the voice, and the trumpet? First Corinthians 15:52 indicates that this will happen so suddenly that it will be over in he twinkling of an eye. Since the shout, voice, and trumpet apply to God's people, there is no reason to believe that the unsaved masses will hear them. If they do, they will hear sounds without meanings (see John 12:27-30). Millions of people will vanish instantly, and no doubt there will be chaos and great concern. Except for those who know the Bible teaching, the world will wonder at what has happened.

Reunion: Christians Forever with the Lord (4:17-18)

You and I shall meet the Lord in the air, in person, when He comes for us. The Greek word translated "meet" carries the idea of meeting a royal person or an important person. We have walked with Christ by faith here on earth, but in the air we shall "see Him as He is" and become like Him (1 John 3:1-2). What a meeting that will be!

It will be a *glorious* meeting, because we shall have glorified bodies. When He was here on earth, Jesus prayed that we might one day see His glory and share in it (John 17:22-24). The suffering that we endure today will be transformed into glory when He returns (2 Cor. 4:17-18, and Rom. 8:17-19).

It will be an *everlasting* meeting, for we shall be "forever with the Lord." This was His promise: "I will come again, and receive you unto Myself; that where I am, there ye may be also" (John 14:3). The goal of redemption is not just to rescue us from judgment, but to relate us to Christ.

Our meeting with the Lord will also be a time of *reckoning*. This is called "the Judgment Seat of Christ" (Rom. 14:10 and 2 Cor. 5:10). The Greek word *bema*, which is translated "judgment seat," referred to the place where the Olympic judges awarded crowns to the winners. Our works will be judged and rewards will be given (1 Cor. 3:8-15).

The Judgment Seat of Christ must not be confused with the White Throne Judgment described in Revelation 20:11-15. You may contrast these two important events as follows:

Judgment Seat of Christ	White Throne Judgment
Only believers	Only unbelievers
Immediately after the Rapture	After the thousand-year kingdom

| Determines rewards | Determines amount |
| for service | of judgment |

We will not only meet our Lord Jesus Christ at the Rapture, but will also be reunited with our believing friends and loved ones who have died. "Together with them" is a great statement of encouragement. Death is the great separator, but Jesus Christ is the great Reconciler.

The Bible does not reveal all the details of this reunion. When Jesus raised the widow's son from the dead, He tenderly "delivered him to his mother" (Luke 7:15). This suggests that our Lord will have the happy ministry of reuniting broken families and friendships.

On the Mount of Transfiguration, the three disciples knew and recognized Moses and Elijah (Matt. 17:1-5). Certainly, the saints will know each other in glory, including believers we have never met. "For now we see through a glass, darkly; but then face to face: now I know in part; but then shall I know even as also I am known" (1 Cor. 13:12).

In the next chapter, we will see how Paul related this doctrine of the return of Christ to the unsaved. But it would be good for us now to examine our own hearts to see if we are ready to meet the Lord. One mark of a true Christian is his eager looking for the coming of Jesus Christ (1 Thes. 1:10). As we grow in the Lord, we not only look *for* His appearing, but we *love* His appearing (2 Tim. 4:8). Because we have this hope in Him, we keep our lives pure so that we may not be ashamed at His coming (1 John 2:28—3:3).

Robert Murray McCheyne, the godly Presbyterian preacher, used to ask people: "Do you think

Jesus Christ will return today?" Most of them would reply, "No, not today." Then McCheyne would say, "Then, my friend, you had better be ready; for He is coming at such an hour as ye think not" (Luke 12:40).

Death is a fact of life. The only way we can escape death is to be alive when the Lord Jesus Christ returns. Death is not an accident; it is an appointment: "It is appointed unto men once to die, but after this the judgment" (Heb. 9:27). If you should die today, *where would your soul go?*

I once saw a quaint inscription on a gravestone in an old British cemetery not far from Windsor Castle. It read:

> Pause, my friend, as you walk by;
> As you are now, so once was I.
> As I am now, so you will be.
> Prepare, my friend, to follow me!

I heard about a visitor who read that epitaph and added these lines:

> To follow you is not my intent,
> Until I know which way you went!

We Christians have wonderful assurance and hope, because of the resurrection of Jesus Christ and His promised return.

> Do you have that hope today?
> Which way are *you* going?

¹But of the times and the seasons, brethren, ye have no need that I write unto you. ²For yourselves know perfectly that the Day of the Lord so cometh as a thief in the night. ³For when they shall say, "Peace and safety," then sudden destruction cometh upon them, as travail upon a woman with child; and they shall not escape. ⁴But ye, brethren, are not in darkness, that that day should overtake you as a thief. ⁵Ye are all the children of light, and the children of the day: we are not of the night, nor of darkness. ⁶Therefore let us not sleep, as do others; but let us watch and be sober. ⁷For they that sleep, sleep in the night; and they that be drunken are drunken in the night. ⁸But let us, who are of the day, be sober, putting on the breastplate of faith and love; and for an helmet, the hope of salvation. ⁹For God hath not appointed us to wrath, but to obtain salvation by our Lord Jesus Christ, ¹⁰who died for us, that, whether we wake or sleep, we should live together with Him. ¹¹Wherefore comfort yourselves together, and edify one another, even as also ye do.

1 Thessalonians 5:1-11

8

Don't Walk in Your Sleep!

Jesus Christ both unites and divides. Those who have trusted Him as Saviour are united in Christ as God's children. We are members of His Body and "all one in Christ Jesus" (Gal. 3:28). When Jesus Christ returns in the air, we shall be "caught up together" (1 Thes. 4:17) never to be separated again.

But Christ is also a divider. "So there was a division among the people because of Him" (John 7:43; and see John 9:16 and 10:19). Faith in Jesus Christ not only unites us to other believers; it also separates us spiritually from the rest of the world. Jesus said, "They are not of the world, even as I am not of the world" (John 17:16). There is a difference between believers who are looking for the Lord's return and the people of the world; it is this theme that Paul developed in this section.

His purpose was to encourage the believers to live holy lives in the midst of their pagan surroundings. He did this by pointing out the contrasts between believers and unbelievers.

Knowledge and Ignorance (5:1-2)

Three phrases in these verses need careful consideration.

1. "Times and Seasons." This phrase is found only three times in the Bible, and refers primarily to God's plans for Israel. This is the way Daniel stated it when God gave him understanding of the king's dream (Dan. 2:21). Our Lord's use of the phrase in Acts 1:7 indicates that times and seasons relate primarily to Israel.

God has a definite plan for the nations of the world (Acts 17:26), and Israel is the key nation. Dr. A. T. Pierson used to say, "History is His story." (Quite a contrast to Napoleon's definition: "History is a set of lies agreed upon.") God has ordained times and seasons for the nations on earth, particularly Israel; and all of this will culminate in a terrible time called "the Day of the Lord."

2. "The Day of the Lord." In the Bible, the word *day* can refer to a 24-hour period, or to a longer time during which God accomplishes some special purpose. In Genesis 2:3 the word means 24 hours, but in verse 4 it describes the entire week of Creation.

The Day of the Lord is that time when God will judge the world and punish the nations. At the same time, God will prepare Israel for the return of Jesus Christ to the earth to establish His kingdom. Read Amos 5:18ff; Joel 2:1ff; Zephaniah 1:14-18; and Isaiah 2:12-21 for a description of this great period. *Isa 13:6-13*

Another term for this period is "the time of Jacob's trouble" (Jer. 30:7). Many prophetic students also call it the Tribulation and point to Revelation 6—19 as the Scripture that most vividly describes this event.

3. *"Thief in the night."* Our Lord used this image in His own teaching (Matt. 24:42-43; Luke 12:35-40). It describes the suddenness and the surprise involved in the coming of the Day of the Lord. In Revelation 3:3 and 16:15, He used this image to warn believers not to be caught napping. Since we do not know when the Lord will return for His people, we must live in a constant attitude of watching and waiting, while we are busy working and witnessing.

Now we can put these three concepts together and discover what Paul wanted to teach his troubled friends in Thessalonica. He had already told them about the coming of Christ for the church, the event described in 1 Thessalonians 4:13-18. He had told them that there would be a period of intense suffering and tribulation on the earth following this Rapture of the church. These "times and seasons" that relate to Israel and the nations do not apply to the church or affect the truth of the Lord's coming for the church. He may come at any time, and this will usher in the Day of the Lord.

Paul explained more about the Day of the Lord in his second letter to the Thessalonicans, so we will save these details for a later chapter. His emphasis here was simply that the believers were "in the know" while the unbelievers were living in ignorance of God's plan. The suddenness of these events will reveal to the world its ignorance of divine truth.

Expectancy and Surprise (5:3-5)

The unsaved world will be enjoying a time of false peace and security just before these cataclysmic events occur. Note carefully the contrast between "they" and "you" (or "us") throughout this entire section, "they" referring to the unsaved. *They* will say, "Peace and safety!" but *we* will say, "Jesus is coming, and judgment is coming!"

The world is caught by surprise because men will not hear God's Word or heed God's warning. God warned that the Flood was coming, yet only eight people believed and were saved (1 Peter 3:20). Lot warned his family that the city would be destroyed, but they would not listen (Gen. 19:12-14). Jesus warned His generation that Jerusalem would be destroyed (Luke 21:19ff), and this warning enabled believers to escape; but many others perished in the seige.

In fact, Jesus used the Flood and the overthrow of Sodom and Gomorrah as examples (Matt. 24:37-39 and Luke 17:26-30). People in those days were going about their regular daily activities— eating, drinking, getting married—and never considering that judgment was around the corner.

Well-meaning people have tried to set dates for our Lord's return, only to be embarrassed by their failures. However, it is possible to expect His coming without setting a specific time. No "signs" must be fulfilled before He can return for His church.

Christians are "sons of the light" and therefore are not "in the dark" when it comes to future events. Unbelievers ridicule the idea of Christ's return. "Knowing this first, that there shall come in the last days scoffers, walking after their own lusts, and saying, 'Where is the promise of His coming?'" (2 Peter 3:3-4)

Nearly 20 centuries have come and gone since our Lord gave the promise of His return, and He has not returned yet. This does not mean that God does not keep His promises. It simply means that

God does not follow our calendar. "One day is with the Lord as a thousand years, and a thousand years as one day" (2 Peter 3:8).

Paul compared the coming judgment to "travail upon a woman with child" (1 Thes. 5:3). Even with our modern medical skills, birth pangs are very real and very painful. They accompany the muscle contractions that enable the mother to give birth to the baby. The prophet Isaiah used this same picture when he described the coming "Day of the Lord" (Isa. 13:6-13). The early part of this Day of the Lord was called "the beginning of sorrows" by the Lord Jesus (Matt. 24:8); and the Greek word translated "sorrows" actually means "birth pangs."

What truth do Isaiah, Jesus, and Paul teach us? The truth that out of the Day of the Lord will come the birth of the kingdom. When God's judgments are finished, God's Son will return "with power and great glory" (Matt. 24:30). Paul described this event in his second letter to the Thessalonian Christians.

Live expectantly. This does not mean putting on a white sheet and sitting atop a mountain. That is the very attitude God condemned (Acts 1:10-11). But it does mean living in the light of His return, realizing that our works will be judged and that our opportunities for service on earth will end. It means to live "with eternity's values in view."

There is a difference between being ready to go to heaven and being ready to meet the Lord. Anyone who has sincerely trusted Christ for salvation is ready to go to heaven. Christ's sacrifice on the cross has taken care of that. But to be ready to meet the Lord at the Judgment Seat of Christ is quite another matter. Scripture indicates that some

believers will not be happy to see Jesus Christ!
"And now, little children, abide in Him; that when
He shall appear, we may have confidence, and not
be ashamed before Him at His coming" (1 John
2:28).

Having been a pastor for many years, I have had
the sad experience of seeing believers deliberately
disobey the Word of God. I recall one young lady
who stubbornly chose to marry an unsaved man.
When I tried to help her from the Bible, she said,
"I don't care what you say. I don't care what the
Bible says. I'm going to get married!" In the light
of Hebrews 13:17, will she be happy at the Judgment Seat of Christ?

Believers who live in the expectation of the
Lord's return will certainly enjoy a better life than
Christians who compromise with the world. At the
end of each chapter in this letter, Paul pointed out
the practical results of living expectantly. Take
time now to review those verses and to examine
your heart.

Soberness and Drunkenness (5:6-8)

To be soberminded means to be alert, to live with
your eyes open, to be sane and steady. To make the
contrast more vivid, Paul pictured two groups of
people: one group was drunk and asleep, while the
other group was awake and alert. Danger was
coming, but the drunken sleepers were unaware of
it. The alert crowd was ready and unafraid.

Since we are "sons of the day" we should not
live as those who belong to the darkness. "The
night is far spent, the day is at hand: let us therefore cast off the works of darkness, and let us put
on the armor of light. Let us walk honestly, as in
the day; not in rioting and drunkenness, not in

chambering [immorality] and wantonness [indecency], not in strife and envying" (Rom. 13:12-13).

In other words, because "the day" is approaching, it is time to wake up, clean up, and dress up. And when we dress up, we had better put on "the breastplate of faith and love: and for a helmet, the hope of salvation" (1 Thes. 5:8). Only the "armor of light" (Rom. 13:12) will adequately protect us in these last days before our Lord returns.

The soberminded believer has a calm, sane outlook on life. He is not complacent, but neither is he frustrated and afraid. He hears the tragic news of the day, yet he does not lose heart. He experiences the difficulties of life, but he does not give up. He knows his future is secure in God's hands, so he lives each day creatively, calmly, and obediently. Outlook determines outcome; and when your outlook is the *uplook*, then your outcome is secure.

But the unsaved people of the world are not alert. They are like drunken men, living in a false paradise and enjoying a false security. When the Holy Spirit filled the first Christians at Pentecost, the unsaved people accused the Christians of being drunk (Acts 2:13). In reality, it is the unsaved who are living like drunken men. The sword of God's wrath hangs over the world; yet people live godless lives, empty lives, and rarely if ever give any thought to eternal matters.

We have met faith, hope, and love before (1:3). Here they are described as armor to protect us in this evil world. Faith and love are like a breastplate that covers the heart: faith toward God, and love toward God's people. Hope is a sturdy helmet that protects the mind. The unsaved fix their minds on the things of this world, while dedicated believers set their attention on things above (Col. 3:1-3).

Hope of salvation does not mean the hope that at last we will be saved. A person can *know today* that he is saved and going to heaven. Paul knew that the Thessalonican believers were saved (1:4), and he was certain that he and they would meet Christ in the air (4:17). The person who confidently says, "I know I am saved!" is not exhibiting pride; he is demonstrating faith in God's Word. First John was written to help us know that we are saved (1 John 5:9-13).

Hope of salvation means "the hope that salvation gives to us." There are actually three tenses to salvation: (1) *past*—I have been saved from the guilt and penalty of sin; (2) *present*—I am being saved from the power and pollution of sin; (3) *future*—I shall be saved from the very presence of sin when Christ returns. The blessed hope of our Lord's return is the "hope of salvation." Unsaved people are without hope (Eph. 2:12). This helps explain why they live as they do: "Eat, drink, and be merry, for tomorrow we die!"

Paul repeated the word *sleep* several times in these verses to describe the attitude of the lost world. In the previous paragraph (4:13-18) Paul used the word to describe the death of the believer. The body goes to sleep and the spirit goes to be with the Lord. But in this section, sleep does not mean death. It means moral indifference and carelessness about spiritual things. Jesus used the word "sleep" with this meaning in Mark 13:32-37.

Doctors tell us that some people are "morning people" while others are "evening people." That is, some people are wide awake before the alarm clock rings. They hit the floor running, and never have to yawn or throw cold water in their face. Others (like myself) wake up slowly—first one eye, then the other—and then gradually shift gears as they move into the day. When it comes to the return of our Lord, we must all be "morning people"—awake, alert, sober, and ready for the dawning of that wonderful new day.

But, for the unsaved crowd, revelling in its drunkenness, the coming of Jesus Christ will mean the end of light and the beginning of eternal darkness.

Salvation and Judgment (5:9-11)

Believers do not have to fear future judgment because it is not part of God's appointed plan for us. Will Christians go through the Day of the Lord, that awful period of judgment that God will send upon the earth? I think not, and verses like 1 Thessalonians 1:10 and 5:9 seem to support this. Christians have always gone through tribulation, since this is a part of dedicated Christian living (John 15:18-27 and 16:33). But they will not go through *the* Tribulation that is appointed for the godless world.

I realize that good and godly students of the Word disagree on this matter, and I will not make it a test of fellowship or spirituality. But I do believe that the church will be raptured to heaven prior to the Tribulation period. Let me share the reasons that have convinced me.

1. The nature of the church. The church is the body of Christ, and He is the Head (Col. 2:17-19). When He died for us on the cross, He bore for us all the divine judgment necessary for our salvation. He has promised that we shall never taste any of

God's wrath (John 5:24). The Day of the Lord is a day of God's wrath, and it seems unjust and unnecessary that the church should experience it.

2. The nature of the tribulation. This is the time when God will judge the Gentile nations and also purge Israel and prepare her for the coming of her Messiah. The "earth-dwellers" will taste of God's wrath (Rev. 3:10) and not those whose citizenship is in heaven (Phil. 3:20). God will judge the earth-dwellers for their iniquity (Isa. 26:20-21). But He has already judged believers' sins on the cross.

3. The promise of Christ's imminent return. The word *imminent* means "ready to happen." Nothing has to occur for Christ to return, except the calling out of the last person who will be saved and complete the body of Christ. If our Lord did not return for us until the end of the Tribulation period, then we would know *when* He was coming; for the sequence, signs, and times are all spelled out in Revelation 6—19. It is worth noting that the word *church* is not used in Revelation from 4:1 to 22:13. Also notice that Paul lived in the expectation of seeing Christ, for he used the pronouns *we* and *us* in discussing this doctrine (1 Thes. 4:13—5:11). The Apostle John had this same attitude. He closed his book with the prayer, "Even so, come, Lord Jesus" (Rev. 22:20).

4. The course of the seven churches in Revelation 2—3. Many Bible students believe the Lord selected these seven churches to illustrate the spiritual course of church history. Ephesus would be the church of the apostles; Smyrna would be the persecuted church of the early centuries. The last church, Laodicea, represents the apostate church of the Last Days.

This suggests that the Philadelphia church (Rev.

3:7-13) pictures the weak but faithful church of the period just before Christ returns. It is an evangelistic church with great opportunities and open doors. It is the church that proclaims the soon-coming of Christ ("Thou has kept the word of My patience" Rev. 3:10), and to it He has promised deliverance from the day of judgment: "I also will keep thee from the hour of temptation, which shall come upon all the world, to try them that dwell upon the earth" (Rev. 3:10). This promise parallels the promise of 1 Thessalonians 5:9.

5. *The order of events in 2 Thessalonians 2.* We will study this in detail in a later chapter, but notice that the order Paul uses harmonizes with the order indicated in other prophetic Scriptures.

Paul connected the return of Christ with the redemption He purchased for us on the cross. We are "bought with a price." We are His bride, and He will come to claim us for Himself before He sends judgment on the earth. Remember that Christ died for us that we might live *through* Him (1 John 4:9), *for* Him (2 Cor. 5:15), and *with* Him (1 Thes. 5:10). Whether we live or die ("wake or sleep"), we are the Lord's and we shall live with Him.

We must never permit the study of prophecy to become purely academic, or a source of tension or argument. Paul closed this section with the practical application of the prophetic Scriptures: *encouragement* and *edification.* The fact that we will meet our loved ones again and forever be with the Lord is a source of encouragement (1 Thes. 4:18); and the fact that we will not endure God's wrath during the Day of the Lord is another source of encouragement (1 Thes. 5:11). The first is positive, and the second is negative, and both are comforting.

The truth of our Lord's imminent return encourages us to keep clean (1 John 3:1-3) and to do faithfully whatever work He has assigned to us (Luke 12:41-48). It also encourages us to attend church and love the brethren (Heb. 10:25). Knowing that we shall be with the Lord strengthens us in the difficulties of life (2 Cor. 5:1-8) and motivates us to win the lost (2 Cor. 5:9-21).

Many believers have such a comfortable situation here on earth that they rarely think about going to heaven and meeting the Lord. They forget that they must one day stand at the Judgment Seat of Christ. It helps to hold us up and builds us up when we recall that Jesus is coming again.

If you have never trusted Him, then your future is judgment. You needn't be ignorant, for God's Word gives you the truth. You needn't be unprepared, for today you can trust Christ and be born again. Why should you live for the cheap sinful experiences of the world when you can enjoy the riches of salvation in Christ?

If you are not saved, then you have an appointment with judgment. And it may come sooner than you expect, for it is "appointed unto men once to die, but after this the judgment" (Heb. 9:27). Why not make an "appointment" with Christ, meet Him personally, and trust Him to save you? "For whosoever shall call upon the name of the Lord shall be saved" (Rom. 10:13).

¹²And we beseech you, brethren, to know them which labor among you, and are over you in the Lord, and admonish you; ¹³and to esteem them very highly in love for their work's sake. And be at peace among yourselves. ¹⁴Now we exhort you, brethren, warn them that are unruly, comfort the feebleminded, support the weak, be patient toward all men. ¹⁵See that none render evil for evil unto any man; but ever follow that which is good, both among yourselves, and to all men. ¹⁶Rejoice evermore. ¹⁷Pray without ceasing. ¹⁸In every thing give thanks: for this is the will of God in Christ Jesus concerning you. ¹⁹Quench not the Spirit. ²⁰Despise not prophesyings. ²¹Prove all things; hold fast that which is good. ²²Abstain from all appearance of evil. ²³And the very God of peace sanctify you wholly; and I pray God your whole spirit and soul and body be preserved blameless unto the coming of our Lord Jesus Christ. ²⁴Faithful is He that calleth you, who also will do it. ²⁵Brethren, pray for us. ²⁶Greet all the brethren with an holy kiss. ²⁷I charge you by the Lord that this epistle be read unto all the holy brethren. ²⁸The grace of our Lord Jesus Christ be with you. Amen.

1 Thessalonians 5:12-28

9

It's All in the Family

Paul's favorite name for believers was *brethren*. He used it at least 60 times in his letters; and in the two Thessalonian Epistles, he used it 27 times. Paul saw the local church as a family. Each member was born again by the Spirit of God and possessed God's nature (1 Peter 1:22-25; 2 Peter 1:3-4). They all were part of God's family.

It is tragic when believers neglect or ignore the local church. No family is perfect and no local church is perfect; but without a family to protect him and provide for him, a child would suffer and die. The child of God needs the church family if he is to grow, develop his gifts, and serve God.

What are the essentials for a happy, thriving church family? How can we make our local churches more spiritual to the glory of God? In this closing section, Paul discussed these matters

Family Leadership (5:12-13)
Without leadership, a family falls apart. The father is the head of the home; the mother stands with

him in love and cooperation. The children are to obey their parents. This is the order God has laid down, and for us to disturb this order is to ask for serious trouble.

According to Martin L. Gross in his book, *The Psychological Society,* more than 60,000 guidance workers and 7,000 school psychologists work in our American public education system; and many of them function as substitute parents. Many students need counseling, but no professional worker can take the place of a loving, faithful father or mother.

When our oldest son entered high school, he met his assigned counselor. "Now, if you have any problems, feel free to come to me," the counselor said. Our son replied, "If I have any problems, I'll talk to my father!" He was not being disrespectful or unappreciative of the counselor, but he was giving expression of a basic principle: children need the leadership and guidance that only parents can give.

God has ordained leadership for the local church. It is true that we are "all one in Christ Jesus" (Gal. 3:28); but it is also true that the Head of the church has given gifts to people, and then given these people to the churches to exercise His will (Eph. 4:7-16). Just as the flock needs a shepherd (1 Peter 5:1-5), so the family needs a leader.

What responsibilities do the brethren have toward their spiritual leaders?

1. Accept them. They are God's gifts to the church. They have spiritual authority from the Lord and we should accept them in the Lord. They are not dictators, but leaders and examples. As they follow the Lord, we must follow them.

2. Appreciate them. That is the meaning of the exhortation "know them who labor among you"

(1 Thes. 5:12). There is nothing wrong with honoring faithful servants of God, so long as God gets the glory. Spiritual leadership is a great responsibility and a difficult task. It is not easy to serve as a pastor, elder, deacon, or other spiritual leader. The battles and burdens are many, and sometimes the encouragements are few. It is dangerous when a church family takes their leaders for granted and fails to pray for them, work with them, and encourage them.

3. *Love them.* As brothers, the leaders are "among us;" and as leaders, they are "over us in the Lord." This could be a very strained relationship apart from true Christian love. For a pastor to be "among" and "over" at the same time demands grace and the power of the Spirit. If he gets out of balance, his ministry will be weakened and possibly destroyed. Some church members want their pastor to be a buddy, but this weakens his authority. On the other hand, if he emphasizes *only* his authority, he could become a selfish dictator.

4. *Obey them.* "Obey them that have the rule over you, and submit yourselves" (Heb. 13:17). When God's servant, led by God's Spirit, calls us to obey God's Word, then we must obey. This does not mean that every spiritual leader is always right in everything. Abraham, Moses, David, and even Peter, made mistakes in their words and deeds. A wise pastor knows he is made of clay and admits when he is wrong or when he needs expert counsel. In my own ministry, I have benefited tremendously from the counsel and help of experienced laymen whose knowledge in many areas was far greater than mine.

But, in spite of their limitations, God's spiritual

leaders should be respected and obeyed—unless it is obvious that they are out of God's will. As the spiritual leaders of the church meet together, plan, pray, and seek and follow God's will, we can be sure that God will rule and overrule in the decisions they make.

The result of the church family following the spiritual leaders will be peace and harmony in the church: "And be at peace among yourselves" (5:13). Whenever you find division and dissension in a local church, it is usually because of selfishness and sin on the part of the leaders, or the members, or both. James 4:1-3 makes it clear that selfishness on the inside leads to strife on the outside. It is only as we submit to one another in the Lord that we can enjoy His blessing, and peace in the family.

But the leaders alone cannot do all of the work of the ministry; so Paul added a second essential.

Family Partnership (5:14-16)

In recent years, churches have rediscovered what we are calling body-life. This is a scriptural concept, although it does not define all that is involved in the ministry of the local church, since there are other pictures of the church besides that of the body. Body-life refers to the ministry of each Christian to the others, just as the various members of the human body minister to one another to maintain health and life.

Family members must learn to minister to each other. The older members teach the younger members (see Titus 2:3-5) and encourage them when they are in difficulty. While ministering at a summer Bible conference, my wife and I met a lovely Christian couple who had nine children. It was a delight to see how the older children helped the younger ones, and how the parents were relieved of minor tasks and able to enjoy their leisure time.

According to Ephesians 4:12, the spiritual leaders in the church are supposed to equip the members to do the work of the ministry. In most churches, the members pay the leaders to do the work of the ministry; and the leaders cannot do it all. Consequently, the work begins to weaken and die, and everybody blames the preacher.

Paul named some special family members who need personal help.

1. *The unruly (5:14).* This word means "careless, out of line." It was applied to a soldier who would not keep rank but insisted on marching his own way. While the loving atmosphere of the family encourages individual development, there are some things we all must do in the same way. If we do not have rules and standards in the family, we have chaos. Paul dealt with this problem again when he wrote his second epistle to the Thessalonians (3:6, 11), so apparently this first admonition did not impress them.

Rules and traditions in a family must never be so overemphasized that creativity is stifled. As a parent, it is a joy to see each child blossom out with his own personality, talents, and ambitions. But it is a sorrow to see a child rebel against the rules, abandon the traditions and standards, and think that this kind of life-style shows freedom and maturity. This kind of attitude in the church family causes arguments and splits.

2. *The feebleminded (5:14).* This term has nothing to do with mentality. The literal translation of the Greek word is "little-souled, fainthearted." These are the quitters in the church family. They always look on the dark side of things and give up

when the going is tough. In families where there are three or more children, usually one of them is a quitter. Every church family has its share of quitters too.

These people need to be encouraged, which is the meaning of the word translated "comfort" in the King James Version. It is also found in 1 Thessalonians 2:11. The Greek word is made up of two words: *para,* near; and *muthos,* speech. Instead of scolding the fainthearted from a distance, we must get close to them and speak tenderly. We must teach the "little-souled" that the trials of life will help to enlarge them and make them stronger in the faith.

3. *The weak (5:14).* "Hold fast to the weak!" is the literal translation. "Don't let them fall!" But who are these weak believers? Certainly, Paul did not mean people who were weak physically, since he was dealing with the spiritual ministry in the church. No, he was referring to those who were "weak in the faith" and had not grown strong in the Lord (Rom. 14:1—15:3).

Usually, the weak Christians were afraid of their liberty in Christ. They lived by rules and regulations. In the Roman assemblies, the weak Christians would not eat meat, and they held to the Jewish system of holy days. They were severe in their judgment of the mature saints who enjoyed all foods and all days.

We have the strong and the weak in our church families today, just as in our natural families we have children who mature faster than others. How should we handle them? *With patient, reassuring love.* It is unfair and unwise to compare one child with another, for each one matures in his own time and his own way. We must "take hold" of these weaker believers and help them stand and walk in the Lord.

This kind of personal ministry is not easy, and so Paul added some wise counsel to encourage us.

a. Be patient (5:14). It takes patience to raise a family. That weaker member who demands much help may one day be a choice leader, so never give up. A pastor friend and I were chatting after I had spoken at a service in his church, when a red-headed boy about 10 years old came running past us, heading up the center aisle. "Have you ever noticed," remarked my friend, "that the biggest scamps in the Sunday School usually turn out to be pastors or missionaries?" Patience!

b. Watch your motives (5:15). Often as we minister to others, they reject us and even oppose us. Often they show no appreciation. But we should always serve in love, and be ready to forgive. "Never pay back evil for evil to anyone. Respect what is right in the sight of all men. If possible, so far as it depends on you, be at peace with all men. Never take your own revenge, beloved, but leave room for the wrath of God, for it is written, 'Vengeance is Mine, I will repay, says the Lord.' 'But if your enemy is hungry, feed him, and if he is thirsty, give him a drink; for in so doing you will heap burning coals upon his head.' Do not be overcome by evil, but overcome evil with good" (Rom. 12:17-21, NASB).

If your motive is a desire for appreciation and praise, you may be disappointed. If your motive is "ourselves your servants for Jesus' sake" (2 Cor. 4:5), you will never be disappointed.

c. Be joyful (5:16). Joy takes the burden out of service. "The joy of the Lord is your strength" (Neh. 8:10). God loves a cheerful servant as well as a cheerful giver. Every church family has its Doubting Thomas or its Gloomy Gus. To see them and listen to them is like witnessing an autopsy, or diving into a cold lake on a winter's day. God wants His family to be happy, and that means that each member must contribute to the joy.

The four spiritual characteristics Paul mentioned are part of the fruit of the Spirit named in Galatians 5:22—love (v. 13), joy (v. 16), peace (v. 13), and long-suffering (v. 14). We cannot manufacture these spiritual qualities; they only come as we yield to the Spirit and permit Him to control us.

Family partnership is vital to the health and growth of the church. Are you bearing your share of the burdens, or are you merely a spectator who watches the others do the job?

Family Worship (5:17-28)

Worship is the most important activity of a local church family. Ministry must flow out of worship, otherwise it becomes busy activity without power and without heart. There may be "results," but they will not glorify God or really last. Many church services lack an emphasis on true worship and are more like religious entertainments, catering to the appetites of the congregation.

Paul named the various elements that make up the worship ministry of the church.

1. Prayer (5:17). Prayer was important in the early church (1 Cor. 11:1-6; Acts 1:13-14; and 4:23ff.). It was a high and holy experience when the church united in prayer. Today we "call someone to lead in prayer," and we have no idea whether that believer is even in fellowship with God. In some churches, there are two or three people who monopolize the prayer meeting. If we are led by the Spirit (Jude 20), we will experience unity and freedom in our praying, and God will answer.

"Pray without ceasing" does not mean we must always be mumbling prayers. The word means "constantly recurring," not continuously occurring. We are to "keep the receiver off the hook" and be in touch with God so that our praying is part of a long conversation that is not broken. God knows the desires of the heart (Ps. 37:4), and He responds to those desires even when our voice is silent. See Psalms 10:17 and 21:2.

2. Praise (5:18). Thanksgiving is also a vital element of worship. We use "psalms and hymns and spiritual songs" (Eph. 5:19) to express our love and gratitude to the Lord. As we grow in our application of the Word of God, we must also grow in our expression of praise, for the two go together (Col. 3:16). If a local church is "growing in grace" the members will want to learn new hymns in order to give praise to God. If the heart and head do not keep pace with each other, Christian worship becomes either juvenile or hypocritical.

3. The Word of God (5:19-21). Apart from God's Word, we have no certain revelation from the Lord. Worship that ignores the Bible is not spiritual. There may be emotion—and even commotion—but unless there is *spiritual truth,* the Holy Spirit is not at work. The three admonitions in these verses go together and help us understand how the Holy Spirit works in Christian worship.

The early church did not have a completed Bible as we do. The Holy Spirit gave the gift of prophecy to certain members of the church and would speak the message through them. When I preach in a church service, I preach the truth *mediately* by means of the Bible. These early prophets preached the truth *immediately* as they were moved by the Holy Spirit. Their spiritual knowledge was given to them by the Spirit, and often they spoke in a tongue. This is why the three gifts of prophecy, tongues, and knowledge are grouped together in 1 Corinthians 13.

Of course, there are dangers in this kind of ministry; because Satan (or the flesh) could seek to counterfeit a message from God, and thus lead the church astray. If the church restrained the speakers, they might be guilty of quenching the Spirit. If they believed all that was spoken, they might be obeying false spirits. The answer was to "Prove all things." There must be a discerning of the spirits (1 Cor. 12:10; 1 John 4:1-4). Paul gave specific rules for this in 1 Corinthians 14:29-33.

Today, we have a completed revelation in the Word of God and there is no need for prophets. The apostles and prophets helped lay the foundation of the church (Eph. 2:20) and have now passed from the scene. The only "prophetic ministry" we have is in the preaching and teaching of the Word of God.

In using the word *quench*, Paul pictured the Spirit of God as fire. (See Isa. 4:4; Acts 2:3; Rev. 4:5.) Fire speaks of purity, power, light, warmth, and (if necessary) destruction. When the Holy Spirit is at work in our lives and churches, we have a warmth of love in our hearts, light for our minds, and energy for our wills. He "melts us together" so that there is harmony and cooperation; and He purifies us so that we put away sin.

The fire of the Spirit must not go out on the altar of our hearts; we must maintain that devotion to Christ that motivates and energizes our lives.

"Stir up the gift of God which is in thee" Paul wrote to Timothy (2 Tim. 1:6), and the verb means "stir the fire again into life." Apparently Timothy had been neglecting this gift (1 Tim. 4:14) and had to be reminded. The believer, and the local assembly, must avoid extremes: the legalist and formalist would put the fire out, while the fanatic would permit the fire to burn up everything.

It is important that we permit the Spirit of God to teach us the Word of God when we meet to worship. "Sharing" is good if you have something relevant to share from the Word; but I have listened to some "sharing meetings" that were not only unspiritual, but anti-spiritual. "Apt to teach" requires that we be "apt to learn." Beware of a false spirit that can lead you and your church astray. Follow the Word of God and prove all things.

4. Godly living (5:22-24). The purpose of worship is that we might become more like Christ in character and conduct. The greatest definition of worship I ever read was given by William Temple, a late Archbishop of Canterbury: "For to worship is to quicken the conscience by the holiness of God, to feed the mind with the truth of God, to purge the imagination by the beauty of God, to open up the heart to the love of God, to devote the will to the purpose of God."

Paul emphasized balance in Christian living: the negative—"Abstain from all appearance of evil" (v. 22) and the positive—"And the very God of peace sanctify you" (v. 23). Some churches only preach the negative, and this leads to lives and ministries that are out of balance. *Sanctify* simply means "set apart for God's exclusive use." There is *positional* sanctification (Heb. 10:10); we have once and for all been set apart for God. There is also *practical* sanctification (2 Cor. 7:1), a daily dealing with our sins and a growth in holiness. All of this will culminate in *perfect* sanctification (1 John 3:2), when we see Christ and become eternally like Him. Expecting to see Jesus Christ is a great motivation for holy living.

5. *Christian fellowship (5:25-28).* After the corporate worship is ended, the saints minister to one another. They greet one another and seek to encourage. I have been in churches where the congregation escaped like rats leaving a sinking ship. Fellowship is a part of worship.

The "holy kiss" was not a sensual thing. Usually the men kissed the men, and the women kissed the women. (See Rom. 16:16; 1 Cor. 16:20; 1 Peter 5:14.) Often when ministering on mission fields, I have had the saints greet me in this way; and I have never been offended or suspicious. J. B. Phillips in his paraphrase solves the problem by saying, "Give a handshake all around among the brotherhood."

Paul ended with another reminder that the Word of God is the important thing in the local church. The Word must govern our conduct and guide our lives. We are to read the Word personally, but we also need to hear the Word in the fellowship of the local church, for the one experience helps balance the other.

¹Paul, and Silvanus, and Timotheus, unto the church of the Thessalonians in God our Father and the Lord Jesus Christ: ²Grace unto you, and peace, from God our Father and the Lord Jesus Christ. ³We are bound to thank God always for you, brethren, as it is meet, because that your faith groweth exceedingly, and the charity of every one of you all toward each other aboundeth; ⁴so that we ourselves glory in you in the churches of God for your patience and faith in all your persecutions and tribulations that ye endure: ⁵which is a manifest token of the righteous judgment of God, that ye may be counted worthy of the kingdom of God, for which ye also suffer: ⁶seeing it is a righteous thing with God to recompense tribulation to them that trouble you; ⁷and to you who are troubled, rest with us, when the Lord Jesus shall be revealed from heaven with His mighty angels, ⁸in flaming fire taking vengeance on them that know not God, and that obey not the Gospel of our Lord Jesus Christ: ⁹who shall be punished with everlasting destruction from the presence of the Lord, and from the glory of His power; ¹⁰when He shall come to be glorified in His saints, and to be admired in all them that believe (because our testimony among you was believed) in that day. ¹¹Wherefore also we pray always for you, that our God would count you worthy of this calling, and fulfill all the good pleasure of His goodness, and the work of faith with power: ¹²that the name of our Lord Jesus Christ may be glorified in you, and ye in Him, according to the grace of our God and the Lord Jesus Christ.

2 Thessalonians 1:1-12

10

No Rest
for the Wicked

The Christians in Thessalonica were grateful to
God for Paul's letter, but it did not immediately
solve all their problems. In fact, the persecution
grew worse and some believers thought they were
living in the time of the Tribulation. Then a letter
arrived claiming to be from Paul, stating that the
Day of the Lord was actually present. Needless to
say, the assembly was confused and frightened by
this prospect.

Some of the believers concluded that since the
Lord's coming was so near, they ought to quit their
jobs and spend their time waiting for Him. This
meant that the other members were under an extra
burden to care for them. Satan was working over-
time; as the lion, he was seeking to devour (1 Peter
5:7-8), and as the serpent, he was seeking to deceive (2 Cor. 11:3).

It was in response to these needs that Paul wrote
his second letter. (For a suggested outline, see
chapter 1.) He began with their most pressing
need, the persecution they were experiencing be-

cause of their faith. In this first chapter, Paul shared three encouragements with his suffering friends.

The Encouragement of Praise (1:1-4)

After greeting his friends, Paul launched into a statement of praise to God for what He had been accomplishing in their lives. Paul was practicing his own admonition, "In everything give thanks" (1 Thes. 5:18). You cannot help but notice Paul's repeated thanksgivings in these two letters (1 Thes. 1:2; 2:13; 3:9; 2 Thes. 1:3; 2:13). Not only does *prayer* change people and situations, but so does *praise*.

Once I was teaching a series of lessons in a church about Satan's devices to defeat Christians. One of these devices is suffering, as in the case of Job. If Satan can put us into difficult circumstances, he may be able to weaken our faith.

"One of the best weapons for fighting Satan is praise," I told my morning class. "In spite of his pain, Job was able to say, 'Blessed be the name of the Lord!' So, the next time things go wrong and you are tempted to get impatient, turn to God and give thanks."

That evening, just before the class started, a lady rushed up to me and said, "It works! It works!" And then she told me about her afternoon and all that had happened. Her story was so unbelievable that I would have doubted it, had I not known her character. "But in it all I gave thanks," she told me, "and God gave me the grace and strength I needed. It works. Praise works!"

No doubt the Thessalonian believers did not consider themselves to be very spiritual as they suffered, but Paul detected what God was doing among them. You and I are the worst ones to evaluate our own lives. Many times others can see the spiritual improvement when you and I miss it completely. For what blessings did Paul give thanks and thereby encourage his friends?

1. Their faith was growing (1:3a). A faith that cannot be tested cannot be trusted. New believers must expect their faith to be tried, because this is the way God proves whether or not their decision is genuine. Faith, like a muscle, must be exercised to grow stronger. Tribulation and persecution are God's ways to strengthen our faith.

One of my favorite books is *Hudson Taylor's Spiritual Secret,* by Dr. and Mrs. Howard Taylor. In it you read how Hudson Taylor's faith in God grew from that first day he determined to live by faith in God alone. He learned to trust God for his salary, especially when his busy employer forgot to pay him. He learned to trust God for daily needs; and, as his faith was tested, he grew in faith and was able to trust God for His supply for an entire missionary organization. Sometimes it seemed that God had forgotten, but Taylor continued to pray and trust, and God answered.

An easy life can lead to a shallow faith. The great men and women of faith in Hebrews 11 all suffered in one way or another, or faced tremendous obstacles, so that their faith could grow. Paul had prayed for the believers in Thessalonica, that their faith might be perfected (1 Thes. 3:10); and now he thanked God for answered prayer.

2. Their love was abounding (1:3b). Again, this was an answer to Paul's previous prayer (1 Thes. 3:12). Suffering can make us selfish; but when suffering is mixed with grace and faith, it produces love. It is "faith which worketh by love" (Gal. 5:6). When Christians suffer, their faith reaches *upward* to God, and their love reaches *outward* to their fellow believers.

Thoreau once described a city as a place where many people are "lonely together." Residents of a high-rise apartment can be suffering greatly and the people in the next apartment know nothing about it. Our modern world can promote spiritual and emotional isolation and insulation, even to the point of our watching others suffer without really caring.

But for the Christian, suffering can help to produce abounding love. "Behold, how they love one another!" was the confession of the pagan world as it beheld the miracle of Christian fellowship. The early believers were only obeying the commandment of their Lord, "Love one another." Their own suffering did not prevent them from sharing love with others who were suffering.

3. *Their patience was increasing (1:4).* Perhaps "perseverance" would be the best translation of this Greek word. "Tribulation works out endurance" (Rom. 5:3, literal translation). You do not become patient and persevering by reading a book (even this one) or listening to a lecture. *You have to suffer.*

What were these believers enduring? Paul used several words to describe their situation: *persecutions,* which means "attacks from without," or "trials;" *tribulations,* which literally means "pressures," or afflictions that result from the trials; and *trouble* (v. 7), which means "to be pressed into a narrow place." No matter how we look at it, the Thessalonican Christians were not having an easy time.

But God never wastes suffering. Trials work *for* us, not *against* us (James 1:1-5; 2 Cor. 4:15-18). If we trust God and yield to Him, then trials will produce patience and maturity in our lives. If we rebel and fight our circumstances, then we will remain immature and impatient. God permits trials that He might build character into our lives. He can grow a mushroom overnight, but it takes many years—and many storms—to build a mighty oak.

4. Their testimony was helping others (1:4a). "Therefore, among God's churches we boast about your perseverance and faith" (1:4, NIV). Not only can suffering help us to grow, but we can then help others to grow. God encourages us that we may encourage others (2 Cor. 1:4-5). We are not to be cisterns that receive and keep, but channels that receive and direct.

The word translated "faith" in 1:3 and 4, can be translated "faithfulness." Actually, the two go together; we reveal our faith in God by our faithfulness of life. The Thessalonians were faithful to the Lord and to one another, in spite of the troubles they endured. When a person in difficulty forsakes the Lord and the church, he shows that either he has never been born again, or that his spiritual life is very weak. A true Christian who is growing will be faithful, come what may.

During World War II, when enemy armies invaded North Africa, the missionaries had to flee; and there was great concern over the churches left behind. But when the war ended and the missionaries returned, they discovered strong, thriving churches. The sufferings of war purified the church and helped strengthen the faith of the true believers. What an encouragement this was to the churches of the free world.

Paul had every reason to praise God and give thanks for what God was doing in the lives of these young Christians. But did you notice that one element was missing—hope? "Faith, hope, and love" had characterized these believers from the beginning (1 Thes. 1:3); but Paul gave thanks only for their faith and love. Why? Apparently they were confused about their hope. This leads us to the second encouragement.

The Encouragement of Promise (1:5-10)

No matter how difficult their present circumstances may have been, the Thessalonican believers had a secure and glorious future. In fact, their sufferings were evidence, "a manifest token," that God was righteous, working out His great plan for them. We are prone to think that suffering proves that God does not care, when just the opposite is true. Furthermore, the way we act in times of trial proves to others that God is at work. (See Phil. 1:28-30 for another example of this principle.)

Three experiences are involved in the promises of God for His people.

1. Reward (1:5). "You will be counted worthy of the kingdom of God, for which you are suffering" (NIV). This was one of God's purposes in permitting their suffering. It does not suggest that their suffering earned them the right to go to heaven, because we know that they were saved through faith in Christ (1 Thes. 1). The little word "also" indicated that this worthiness related both to their present experience and their future entrance into God's glorious kingdom. You find the same idea in 1 Peter 1:3-9.

One day Jesus Christ will turn the tables and the wicked will suffer while the believers are rewarded. Our Lord never promised us that life here would be easy; in fact, He taught that we would

Promised Land

have to face difficulties and fight battles. But He also promised a future reward for all who were faithful to Him (Matt. 5:10-12).

2. Recompense (1:6-10). God will recompense affliction to the lost, but rest to the saved. *To recompense* means "to repay." Certainly, the wicked who persecute the godly do not always receive their just payment in this life. In fact, the apparent prosperity of the wicked and difficulty of the godly have posed a problem for many of God's people (see Ps. 73; Hab. 1; Jer. 12:1). Why live a godly life if your only experience is that of suffering?

As Christians, we must live for eternity and not just for the present. In fact, living "with eternity's values in view" is what makes our Christian life meaningful today. We walk by faith, and not by sight.

This brings to mind the story of the two farmers, one a believer and the other an atheist. When harvest season came, the atheist taunted his believing neighbor because apparently God had not blessed him too much. The atheist's family had not been sick, his fields were rich with harvest, and he was sure to make a lot of money.

"I thought you said it paid to believe in God and be a Christian," said the atheist.

"It does pay," replied the Christian. "But God doesn't always pay His people in September."

What kind of a future does the unbeliever face? Look at the dramatic words Paul used to describe it: tribulation, vengeance, flaming fire, punishment, and everlasting destruction. The Christ-rejecting world will receive from God exactly what it gave to God's people! When God recompenses, He pays in kind; for there is a law of compensation that operates in human history.

Pharaoh tried to drown all the male babies born to the Jews, and his own army was drowned in the Red Sea. Haman plotted to wipe out the Jews, and he and his own sons were wiped out. The advisors of King Darius forced him to arrest Daniel and throw him into a lions' den, but later they themselves were thrown to the lions. The unbelieving Jewish leaders who sacrificed Christ in order to save the nation (see John 11:49-53) in a few years saw their city destroyed and their nation scattered.

It is a *righteous* thing for God to judge sin and condemn sinners. A holy God cannot leave sin unjudged. People who say, "I cannot believe that a loving God would judge sinners and send people to hell" understand neither the holiness of God nor the awfulness of sin. While it is true that "God is love" (1 John 4:8), it is also true that "God is light" (1 John 1:5), and in His holiness He must deal with sin.

A Christian doctor had tried to witness to a very moral woman who belonged to a church that denied the need for salvation and the reality of future judgment. "God loves me too much to condemn me," the patient would reply. "I cannot believe that God would make such a place as a lake of fire."

The woman became ill and the diagnosis was cancer. An operation was necessary. "I wonder if I really should operate," the doctor said to her in her hospital room. "I really love you too much to cut into you and give you pain."

"Doctor," said the patient, "if you really loved me, you would do everything possible to save me. How can you permit this awful thing to remain in my body?"

It was easy then for him to explain that what

cancer is to the body, sin is to the world; and both must be dealt with radically and completely. Just as a physician cannot love health without hating disease and dealing with it, so God cannot love righteousness without hating sin and judging it.

The word *vengeance* must not be confused with *revenge*. The purpose of vengeance is to satisfy God's holy law; the purpose of revenge is to pacify a personal grudge. God does not hold a grudge against lost sinners. Quite the contrary, He sent His Son to die for them, and He pleads with them to return to Him. But if sinners prefer to "know not God, and . . . obey not the Gospel" (v. 8), there is nothing left for God to do but judge them.

This judgment will take place when Jesus Christ returns to the earth with His church and His angels (1:7). This is not the same event described by Paul in 1 Thessalonians 4:13-18. We may contrast these two events:

1 Thessalonians 4:13-18	2 Thessalonians 1
Christ returns in the air	Christ returns to the earth
He comes secretly *for* the church	He comes openly *with* the church
Believers escape the tribulation	Unbelievers experience tribulation, judgment
Occurs at an undisclosed time	Occurs at the end of the tribulation period, the Day of the Lord

3. *Rest (1:7a and 10).* God will recompense tribulation to the lost, but rest to the saved. I believe that the first phrase in verse 7 should be treated as

a parenthesis: "to recompense tribulation to them that trouble you (and to you who are troubled, rest with us) when the Lord Jesus shall be revealed." The saints receive their rest when the Lord returns in the air and catches us up to be with Him.

The word *rest* means "relief, release, not under pressure." It is the opposite of "tribulation." The word describes the releasing of a bowstring. In this life, God's people are pressured, "pressed out of measure" (2 Cor. 1:8), and under the burdens of trial and persecution. But when we see Christ, we will be released. We need not fear fiery wrath and judgment (1 Thes. 1:10 and 5:9), for God has already judged our sins at Calvary.

What kind of future is there for the lost? They face punishment and eternal judgment (1:9), while the saved shall enjoy the rest and glories of heaven. The lost shall be separated from God, while the saved "shall see His face" (Rev. 22:4). Some cultists have tried to dilute the meaning of "everlasting destruction," saying it means either temporary suffering or total annihilation; but both ideas are false. The phrase means "eternal judgment," no matter how men try to twist it or avoid it (see Matt. 25:41).

Paul encouraged his friends with praise and promise; and he had a third encouragement.

The Encouragement of Prayer (1:11-12)

Paul prayed for his converts (1 Thes. 1:2 and 3:10). His "wherefore" in verse 11 means, "And because of all I have just said"—the return of Christ to be glorified in the saints, and to judge the lost. The future prospect of glory motivated the Apostle to pray for the saints. We must never neglect a present responsibility because of a future hope. On the contrary, the future hope must encourage us to be faithful today.

There were four concerns in Paul's prayer.

1. Their worthiness (1:11a). In verse 5, Paul had stated that he wanted them to be worthy of the kingdom when they entered glory in the future. But here he emphasized their present situation. God's calling was in grace and love, and Paul desired that they might live up to that calling. (See 2 Thes. 2:13-14.)

Trials do not make a person; they reveal what a person is made of. When our faith is tried, we are revealing our worth (1 Peter 1:6-9). God certainly knows our hearts even before we are tried, but *we do not know our own hearts.* And others do not know what we are worth. We need to pray that God will build our worth and make us more valuable Christians because of the trials we have endured.

2. Their walk (1:11b). "That by His power He may fulfill every good purpose of yours and every act prompted by your faith" (NIV). Character must lead to conduct. Paul prayed that they might have a resolute will, empowered by God, to do what He wanted them to do. Obedience and service do not spring from human talents and efforts, but from God's power as we trust Him.

Paul had linked faith with *love* (1:3) and *endurance* (1:4), and here he linked it with *power.* If we believe God, we will receive His power in our lives. We cannot be victorious in tribulations if we only trust ourselves; but we can be victorious through trusting Him.

When I travel, I carry an electric razor that can store up the energy and run for perhaps two hours without any outside source of power. It is especially useful when I visit the mission fields.

While preaching for a week at a summer conference, I noticed that my razor was losing power. In fact, one morning it operated so slowly that I was convinced it was broken. Then by evening, it had picked up speed again. A few minutes investigation revealed the problem: I had plugged the razor into a socket that was controlled by a wall switch. When my wife had the desk lamp on, my razor was storing up power; when the light was off, the razor received no power.

That incident taught me a spiritual lesson: it is easy (by force of habit) to trust a source of power without checking to see if the switch is on. Paul was praying that his friends might "have the switch on" and, by their faith, receive the power needed to endure suffering and glorify God.

3. *The witness (1:12).* Jesus Christ will be glorified in His saints when they return with Him (1:10); but He should also be glorified in our lives today. Unbelievers blaspheme His name (1 Peter 4:12ff.), but believers bless His name and seek to glorify it. The amazing thing is that the believer who glorifies Christ is likewise glorified *in Christ,* "glorified in you, and you in Him" (NIV).

How can this be done? "According to the grace of our God and the Lord Jesus Christ" (1:12). Grace and glory go together, as do suffering and glory (see Ps. 84:11; 1 Peter 5:10; Ps. 45:2-3; Rom. 5:2; 2 Cor. 8:19). As we receive His grace, we reveal His glory.

" 'There is no peace,' saith the Lord, 'unto the wicked' " (Isa. 48:22). No rest for the wicked! But there is rest for those who trust Christ and seek to live for His glory. For the Christian, the best is yet to come. We knew that "the sufferings of this present time are not worthy to be compared with the glory which shall be revealed in us" (Rom. 8:18).

¹Now we beseech you, brethren, by the coming of our Lord Jesus Christ and by our gathering together unto Him, ²that ye be not soon shaken in mind, or be troubled, neither by spirit, nor by word, nor by letter as from us, as that the Day of Christ is at hand. ³Let no man deceive you by any means: for that day shall not come, except there come a falling away first, and that man of sin be revealed, the son of perdition; ⁴who opposeth and exalteth himself above all that is called God, or that is worshiped; so that he as God sitteth in the temple of God, shewing himself that he is God. ⁵Remember ye not, that, when I was yet with you, I told you these things? ⁶And now ye know what withholdeth that he might be revealed in his time. ⁷For the mystery of iniquity doth already work: only he who now letteth will let, until he be taken out of the way. ⁸And then shall that wicked be revealed, whom the Lord shall consume with the spirit of His mouth, and shall destroy with the brightness of His coming: ⁹even him, whose coming is after the working of Satan with all power and signs and lying wonders, ¹⁰and with all deceivableness of unrighteousness in them that perish; because they received not the love of the truth, that they might be saved. ¹¹And for this cause God shall send them strong delusion, that they should believe a lie: ¹²that they all might be damned who believed not the truth, but had pleasure in unrighteousness.

2 Thessalonians 2:1-12

11

God's Timetable

The purpose of Bible prophecy is not for us to make a calendar, but to build character. Paul emphasized this fact in both of his Thessalonian letters, and our Lord warned us not to set dates for His coming (Matt. 24:36, 42). Date-setters are usually upsetters, and that is exactly what happened in the Thessalonican assembly.

Someone had deceived the believers into thinking they were already living in the Day of the Lord. The teaching probably first came through a "prophetic utterance" in one of their meetings, and then it was further enhanced by a letter claiming to come from Paul himself. The believers were instantly shaken by this teaching, and continued to be deeply troubled. Had God changed His program? Had not Paul promised them deliverance from the Tribulation? (See 1 Thes. 1:10 and 5:9.)

To calm their hearts and stabilize their faith, Paul explained that they were not in the Day of the Lord. The reason was simple: that Day could not arrive till certain other events had taken place.

Paul then stated for them the prophetic events that make up God's timetable.

The Rapture of the Church (2:1, 6-7)

Paul appealed to them to "calm down" on the basis of the truth he had taught them in his first letter: the Lord would return and catch up His own to meet Him in the air (1 Thes. 4:13-18). This is "the coming of our Lord Jesus Christ and . . . our gathering together unto Him" (v. 1). Not two separated events, but one great event that will occur suddenly and without warning.

Once the church is out of the world, Satan and his forces will unfold their program. The Day of the Lord is the period that follows the rapture of the church. It will be a time of tribulation for the people on earth: Satan and his hosts will be working on earth, and God will send righteous judgments from heaven. Revelation 6—19 describes this period for us.

Why is Satan unable to reveal his "man of sin" sooner? Because God is restraining the forces of evil in the world today. Satan cannot do whatever he wants to do, whenever he pleases. Our sovereign Lord is able to make even the wrath of man to praise Him, and "the remainder of wrath shalt Thou restrain" (Ps. 76:10). In verses 6 and 7, Paul mentioned a restraining force that even today is helping keep everything on schedule.

Who or what is this restrainer? Paul told the Thessalonians when he was teaching them personally, but he did not put this information in either of his letters. This restrainer is now at work in the world and will continue to work till it (or he) is "taken out of the midst" (literal translation of v. 7b).

Notice that in verse 6 Paul referred to this re-straighter in the neuter gender ("what restraineth"), while in verse 7, he used the masculine gender ("he who now hindereth"). The restrainer is a person who is today "in the midst," but will one day be "taken out of the midst."

Many Bible students identify this restrainer as the Holy Spirit of God. Certainly, He is "in the midst" of God's program today, working through the church to accomplish God's purposes. When the church is raptured, the Holy Spirit will not be taken *out of the world* (otherwise nobody could be saved during the Tribulation), but He will be taken *out of the midst* to allow Satan and his forces to go to work. The Holy Spirit will certainly be present on the earth during the Day of the Lord, but He will not be restraining the forces of evil as He is today.

In spite of its weakness and seeming failure, never underestimate the importance of the church in the world. People who criticize the church do not realize that the presence of the people of God in this world gives unsaved people opportunity to be saved. The presence of the church is delaying the coming of judgment. Lot was not a dedicated man, but his presence in Sodom held back the wrath of God (Gen. 19:12-29).

There are two programs at work in the world today: God's program of salvation, and Satan's program of sin, "the mystery of iniquity." God has a timetable for His program, and nothing Satan does can change that timetable. Just as there was a "fulness of the time" for the coming of Christ (Gal. 4:4), so there is a "fulness of the time" for the appearance of Antichrist; and nothing will be off schedule. Once the restraining ministry of the

Spirit of God has ended, the next event can take place.

The Revelation of Antichrist (2:3-5, 8a)

Paul did not use the term *Antichrist* in his letter. This term is used in the New Testament only by John (1 John 2:18, 22; 4:3; 2 John 7). But this is the name we use to identify the last great world dictator whom Paul designated as "that man of sin," "the son of perdition" (v. 3), and "that lawless one" (v. 8, literal translation).

Satan has been at war with God ever since he, as Lucifer, rebelled against God and tried to capture God's throne (Isa. 14:12-15). He tempted Eve in the Garden and, through her, caused Adam to fall (Gen. 3). In Genesis 3:15, God declared war on Satan and his family, "seed," and promised the coming of the Redeemer who would finally and completely defeat Satan.

The Greek prefix *anti* has two meanings: *against,* and *instead of*. Satan not only opposes Christ, but he wants to be worshiped and obeyed *instead of* Christ. Satan has always wanted to be worshiped and served as God (Isa. 14:14; Luke 4:5-8). He will one day produce his masterpiece, the Antichrist, who will cause the world to worship Satan and believe Satan's lies.

Paul had explained all of this to the believers in Thessalonica, referring them, no doubt, to the relevant Scriptures in the Old Testament. We are fortunate to have the entire Bible to study, so we can get the total picture of Antichrist and his career. Prophetic students may not agree on every detail; but the main facts, when they are related, give us the following description of Antichrist in the last days.

1. The peacemaker (Rev. 6:1-2). Certainly, this man will be on the scene before the rapture of the church. He will be a peaceful political leader who unites 10 nations of Europe into a strong power block (see Rev. 17:12-13). The rider on the white horse imitates Christ (Rev. 19:11ff.). He goes forth to conquer peacefully: he has a bow, but no arrows. He will bring a brief time of peace to the world (1 Thes. 5:1-3) before the storm of the Day of the Lord breaks loose.

2. The protector (Dan. 9:24-27). We cannot examine the exciting details of this prophecy, but it is important to note several facts. First, the prophecy applies to Israel, Jerusalem, and the temple, and not to the church. Second, it announces the time when Messiah will come and accomplish certain purposes for the Jewish people. The word *week* refers to a period of 7 years; 70 weeks are equal to 490 years. Note that these 490 years are divided into three parts: 7 weeks or 49 years, during which the city would be rebuilt; 62 weeks or 434 years, at the end of which time Messiah would come and be cut off; 1 week or 7 years, during which a "prince" would have a covenant with Israel.

Notice that *two princes* are involved in this prophecy: Christ, Messiah the Prince (v. 25), and Antichrist, "the prince that shall come" (v. 26). "The people of the prince that shall come" are the Romans; for it was they who destroyed the city and the temple in A.D. 70. The coming Antichrist will belong to a nation that was part of the old Roman Empire.

Finally, note that there is a parenthesis between the 69th and the 70th week. We are now living in that parenthesis. The 69th week ended with the

ministry of Christ. The 70th week will start with
the arrival of Antichrist. He will make a covenant
with Israel to protect her and permit her to rebuild
her temple. This covenant will be for seven years.
He will temporarily solve the Middle East crisis.
Israel will rebuild her temple in peaceful times. It
is the signing of this covenant, not the rapture of
the church, that signals the start of Daniel's 70th
week, that seven-year period known as the Day of
the Lord.

3. *The peace-breaker (Dan. 9:27).* After three
and one-half years, Antichrist will break his covenant with the Jews *and take over their temple.*
This was what Paul termed "the falling away"
(2 Thes. 2:3b). A better translation would be "the
rebellion, the apostasy." Not simply *a* rebellion,
but *the* rebellion. Up to this point, Antichrist has
been a peacemaking leader of 10 European nations,
obligated to protect Israel. But now he reveals his
true character by taking over the Jewish temple
and demanding that the world worship him. (See
Rev. 13.)

Since Antichrist will be energized by Satan, it is
no surprise that he will seek worship; for Satan
has always wanted the worship of the world. There
have been various "apostasies" in church history,
when groups have turned away from God's truth;
but this final rebellion will be the greatest of all.
The man of sin will oppose everything that belongs
to any other religion, true or false. He will organize
a world church that will, by worshiping him, worship Satan.

Our Lord predicted this apostasy; He called it
"the abomination of desolation" (Matt. 24:15), a
clear reference to Daniel 9:27. The world will wonder at this great leader who, with Satan's power,

will perform signs and wonders and deceive the nations.

4. *The persecutor (Rev. 13:15-17).* Most prophetic students agree that the abomination of desolation will occur three and one-half years after the Antichrist makes his covenant with the Jews. (Dan. 9:27—"in the midst of the week" or three and one-half years.) This will usher in a period of intense persecution and tribulation. Jesus said, "For then shall be great tribulation" (Matt. 24:21). Satan will vent his wrath against Israel. He will so control the world's economic system that citizens must bear "the mark of the beast" to be able to buy and sell (Rev. 13:16-17).

People often ask, "Will anybody be saved during the seven-year period?" The answer is, "Yes!" Revelation 7:1-8 states, that 144,000 Jews will be saved (probably as was the Apostle Paul, by a dramatic vision of Christ) and will carry the Gospel to the nations. The Apostle John described a great multitude of Gentiles who will come out of the great Tribulation (Rev. 7:9-17) as converted people. Even though the Holy Spirit will be "out of the midst" as the restraining power, He will still work with redeeming power.

However, it will cost dearly to trust Christ and live for Him during that time. Believers will refuse to bow down to the beast's image and will be slain. They will refuse to wear his mark and thus be unable to get jobs or make purchases. It will be quite a contrast to our situation now when even famous people admit that they are "born again."

5. *The prisoner (Rev. 19:11-21).* Keep in mind that God has a timetable. Satan will not be permitted to control the world forever. Jesus Christ will return "in power and great glory" and take Anti-

christ and his associates prisoner—and also Satan—
and cast them into the bottomless pit (Rev.
20:1-3). This will be the climax of the great battle
of Armageddon (Rev. 16:16) during which the nations of the world unite with Satan to fight Jesus
Christ. This leads to our next event.

The Return of Jesus Christ (2:8-12)

This is His return to the earth in glory and judgment, the event described in 2 Thessalonians 1:5-10
and Revelation 19:11ff. It will occur at the end of
the seven-year Tribulation period when the "mystery of iniquity" (Satan's evil program) will have
ended with the Battle of Armageddon. It is important that we distinguish His rapture of the church
from His return to the earth. The first event is
secret, as the church is caught up to meet Him in
the air. The second event is public, when the church
returns with Him to defeat Satan and his hosts.

1. His judgment of Antichrist (2:8-9). Nobody on
earth will be able to overcome the Antichrist and
his forces, for he is energized by Satan. "Who is
like unto the beast? Who is able to make war with
him?" (Rev. 13:4) Satan will enable his false messiah to perform "power and signs and lying wonders" (2 Thes. 2:9). This, of course, is in imitation
of Jesus Christ who performed "miracles and wonders and signs" (Acts 2:22).

Satan has always been an imitator. There are
false Christians in the world who are really children of the devil (Matt. 13:38; 2 Cor. 11:26). He
has false ministers (2 Cor. 11:13ff) who preach
a false gospel (Gal. 1:6-9). There is even a "synagogue of Satan" (Rev. 2:9), which means a gathering of people who think they are worshiping God
but who are really worshiping the Devil (1 Cor

10:19-21). These false Christians have a counterfeit righteousness that is not the saving righteousness of Christ (Rom. 10:1-3; Phil. 3:4-10). They have a false assurance of salvation that will prove useless when they face judgment (Matt. 7:15-29).

During the apostolic age, miracles were given to verify the message (Heb. 2:1-4). God's chosen apostles used miracles as their credential to prove they were sent by God (2 Cor. 12:12). However, miracles *alone* never prove that a man is sent from God: his message and his character must also be considered. John the Baptist was "a man sent from God" (John 1:6), yet "John did no miracle" (John 10:41).

Satan can perform miracles that seem to rival those of the Lord. This is how he opposed Moses in the court of Pharaoh (Ex. 7:8-12, 20-22; 8:5-7). In the final judgment, some people who performed miracles *in the name of Jesus* will be rejected by the Lord because they were never saved (Matt. 7:21-23). Judas performed miracles, yet he was never born again (John 6:66-71; 13:11, 18).

The purpose of God's miracles was to lead people to the truth; the purpose of Antichrist's miracles will be to lead people to believe his lies. Paul called them "lying wonders" (v. 9), not because the miracles are not real, but because they persuade people to believe Satan's lies. The world would not long follow a leader who practiced cheap trickery. (See Rev. 13:13-14.)

When Jesus Christ returns, He will judge Antichrist by "the spirit of His mouth . . . and the brightness of His coming" (v. 8). The verbs "consume" and "destroy" do not mean annihilate; for Revelation 20:10 indicates that Satan and his associates will be tormented in the lake of fire forever.

You could translate this statement: "whom the Lord Jesus will overthrow with the breath of His mouth, and bring an end to his operations by the outshining of His presence."

As the coming of the Lord for His church draws near, Satan's operations in this world will intensify. (Read 1 Timothy 4 and 2 Timothy 3.) Since Satan is a liar, we must resist him through the truth of God's Word (Eph. 6:17). It was this sword that our Lord used when He defeated Satan in the wilderness (Matt. 4:1-11). Satan is a liar and a murderer (John 8:44). God gives life through His truth; Satan slays with his lies. We are encouraged to know that one day Jesus Christ will completely overthrow Satan and his system.

2. His judgment of the unsaved (2:10-12). We have noted that a great number of Jews and Gentiles will be saved during the seven-year Tribulation period. But the vast majority of the world's population will be lost. Many will die in the terrible judgments that God will send on earth (see Rev. 6:7-8; 8:11; 9:18; 11:13). Others will perish in judgment when Jesus Christ returns and separates the saved from the lost (Matt. 25:31-46).

It is important to note that these people did have opportunity to believe and be saved. God has no delight in judging the lost (Ezek. 33:11). God is "not willing that any should perish, but that all should come to repentance" (2 Peter 3:9). These people will be judged and will suffer forever because they would not receive and believe the truth. In fact, their hearts will be so evil that they will not even have any *love* for the truth. Those who love lies and make lies will be excluded from the heavenly city (Rev. 22:15) and sent to the lake of fire.

In this paragraph, Paul taught a sobering truth: a person can so resist the truth that he finally becomes deluded and has to believe a lie. There can be no neutral ground: either we believe the truth or we believe a lie. To reject the truth means to receive the lie.

Does this mean that God is to blame for a man's rejection of Christ? No more than God was to blame for Pharaoh's spiritual condition when Moses was bringing the plagues on Egypt. Pharaoh heard God's Word and saw God's wonders, yet he refused to bow to God's will. Pharaoh occasionally relented and gave lip service to God's will; but he always resisted in the end and refused to obey God. He hardened his heart so that he could not believe the truth, and this led to God's final judgment of the land of Egypt.

Verse 11 reads literally "that they should believe *the* lie." What is "the lie"? Satan is the liar and has foisted many deceptions on the human race. But there is one "lie" that, from the beginning, has led people astray. Satan first spoke it to Eve: "You shall be as God!" *The lie* is the idea that man is his own God and therefore can do whatever he pleases and better himself by his own human efforts. The process is described in Romans 1:18ff. Note especially verse 25: "Who exchanged the truth of God for the lie, and worshiped and served the creature rather than the Creator" (literal translation).

All of which means that Satan appeals to man's pride. It was pride that turned Lucifer into Satan (Isa. 14:12-15 and Ezek. 28:11-18). It is pride that traps men into doing Satan's will in this world (see 2 Tim. 2:24-26).

A friend told me about a church officer on the

mission field who was causing great problems in the church. Whenever the missionary was in the village, the officer lived a godly life; but no sooner did the missionary leave than the man began to behave as though he were controlled by Satan. Finally the missionary and several church leaders confronted the man in the name of Jesus Christ, and they discovered the truth: Satan was using pride to control the officer's life.

"When I was ordained an elder," the man explained, "I heard a voice say to me, 'Now you are somebody important.' I yielded to that voice, and Satan took over in my life." He confessed his sin, the church prayed, and God delivered him.

"Now you are somebody important!" "Worship and serve the creature rather than the Creator." This is Satan's lie, and I fear it is what rules the world today. God originally made man in His own image. Today, man is making God in his own image.

The people Christ will judge not only do not love the truth, but they have "pleasure in unrighteousness" (v. 12). Read Psalm 50:16-21 for one description of this kind of person, and also Psalm 52. The chief priests actually were *glad* when Judas promised to help them kill Christ (Mark 14:10-11). I mentioned before that this process of believing the lie is described in Romans 1. The closing verse of that section (1:32) states this truth clearly: "Who knowing the judgment of God, that they which commit such things are worthy of death, not only do the same, but have pleasure in them that do them."

Does this mean that those who have heard the Gospel before the rapture of the church cannot be saved after the Rapture? Not necessarily. If that were true, then our witness to the lost is condemning them, should Christ return. However, it does mean that no lost sinner can afford to treat God's truth carelessly or reject God's Son repeatedly. The human heart becomes harder each time the sinner rejects God's truth; and this makes it easier to believe Satan's lies.

How much better it is to follow the example of the Thessalonican believers who received the Word of God "not as the word of men, but as it is in truth, the Word of God" (1 Thes. 2:13). They received the truth and were saved.

Have you received the truth?

[13]But we are bound to give thanks always to God for you, brethren beloved of the Lord, because God hath from the beginning chosen you to salvation through sanctification of the Spirit and belief of the truth: [14]whereunto He called you by our Gospel, to the obtaining of the glory of our Lord Jesus Christ. [15]Therefore, brethren, stand fast, and hold the traditions which ye have been taught, whether by word, or our epistle. [16]Now our Lord Jesus Christ Himself, and God, even our Father, which hath loved us, and hath given us everlasting consolation and good hope through grace, [17]comfort your hearts, and stablish you in every good word and work.

[3:1]Finally, brethren, pray for us, that the Word of the Lord may have free course, and be glorified, even as it is with you: [2]and that we may be delivered from unreasonable and wicked men: for all men have not faith. [3]But the Lord is faithful, who shall stablish you, and keep you from evil. [4]And we have confidence in the Lord touching you, that ye both do and will do the things which we command you. [5]And the Lord direct your hearts into the love of God, and into the patient waiting for Christ.

2 Thessalonians 2:13—3:5

12

Nothing but the Truth

Paul was a balanced Christian who had a balanced ministry; and we see evidence of this as he brought his letter to a close. He moved from prophecy to practical Christian living. He turned from the negative (Satan's lies) to the positive (God's truth), and from warning to thanksgiving and prayer.

We desperately need balanced ministries today. I have attended Bible conferences where the only emphasis was on what Christ *will do* with the Jews in the future, to the total neglect of what He *wants to do* with the church in the present. We must never permit the study of prophecy to be an escape from responsibility today.

Paul's emphasis was on the truth of God's Word, in contrast to Satan's great lie which Paul discussed in the previous section. Every believer had four responsibilities to God's truth.

Believe the Truth (2:13-14)
We have noted Paul's repeated thanksgiving in his letters to this church (1 Thes. 1:2; 2:13; 3:9; 2 Thes.

1:3; 2:13). He gave thanks for the way they responded to God's work in their lives. In these two verses, Paul reviewed the stages in their salvation experience.

1. God loved them (2:13a). Whatever God does for the lost world springs from His eternal love. We must never conceive of His great plan of salvation as an impersonal machine. His salvation is rooted and grounded in His love (John 3:16). God proved this love at the cross where Jesus Christ died for the sins of the world (Rom. 5:8).

2. God chose them (2:13b). It is not love alone that saves us, for God loves the whole world, and yet the whole world is not saved. Love reveals itself in *grace* and *mercy*. God in His grace gives us through Christ what we do not deserve, and God in His mercy does not give what we do deserve— but He gave that to Christ! We dare not explain away God's election of sinners (1 Thes. 1:4; Eph. 1:4; 1 Peter 1:2).

3. God set them apart (2:13c). The word *sanctify* means "to set apart." There is a progressive sanctification that makes us more like Jesus Christ (1 Thes. 5:23). But the sanctification Paul mentioned here refers to the Spirit's work in leading the unbeliever to faith in Christ. "Elect according to the foreknowledge of God the Father, through sanctification of the Spirit" (1 Peter 1:2). It is the work of the Holy Spirit to bring conviction to the sinner (John 16:7-11). Though I did not realize it at the time, as I look back I can see how the Spirit led in bringing me to faith in Christ; and this is the experience of every believer.

4. God called them (2:14). The same God who ordained the end (salvation) also ordained the means to the end ("belief of the truth"). The per-

son who says, "God already has His elect, so there
is no need for us to pray, witness, and send out
missionaries" does not understand divine election.
The greatest encouragement to evangelism is the
knowledge that God has His people who have
been prepared to respond to His Word (read Acts
18:1-11).

In order for God to fulfill His eternal plan, He
sent Paul, Silas, and Timothy to Thessalonica to
preach the Word of God. What was ordained *in
eternity* was accomplished *in time*. God used human instruments to bring the Gospel to the lost;
and by trusting Christ, these people proved their
"election of God" (1 Thes. 1:4). The call of God
went out to the whole city, but it was effective
only in those who believed the truth and trusted
Christ.

It is dangerous to engage in idle speculation
about divine sovereignty and human responsibility.
Both are taught in the Bible. We know that "salvation is of the Lord" (Jonah 2:9), and that lost
sinners can never save themselves. We must admit
that there are *mysteries* to our salvation; but we
can rejoice that there are *certainties* on which we
can rest. We must not use the doctrine of election
to divide the church or disturb the weak, but to
glorify the Lord.

5. *God gave them glory (2:14b).* What began in
eternity past reaches its climax in eternity future:
we share in the glory of God (Rom. 8:29-30; John
17:24). What begins with grace always leads to
glory. This is quite a contrast to the future assigned
to the lost (2 Thes. 1:8-10). Believers already
possess God's glory within (John 17:22; note the
past tense in Rom. 8:30—"glorified"). We are
awaiting Christ's return, and then the glory shall

be revealed (2 Thes. 1:10; Rom. 8:17-19).

When sinners believe God's truth, God saves them. When they believe Satan's lie, and reject the love of the truth, they cannot be saved (2 Thes. 2:10-12). Being neutral about God's truth is a dangerous thing. It has tragic eternal consequences.

Guard the Truth (2:15)

Paul had told them about the *future* rebellion against the truth (2 Thes. 2:3), the great apostasy headed by the Antichrist. But he also warned in his letters that there was a *present* danger, and that the church must guard God's truth and not turn from it. There are repeated warnings about this in the New Testament: 1 John 2:18-24 and 4:1-3; 2 Peter 2; 1 Timothy 4; 2 Timothy 3, to name only a few.

God works in this world through the truth of His Word, and Satan opposes this truth by substituting his lies. Human nature is prone to believe a lie and resist the truth. Satan accomplishes his best work through people in so-called Christian institutions (churches, schools, etc.) who do not believe God's truth. They have "a form of godliness" but have never experienced the power of God's saving truth.

When Paul used the word *traditions,* he was not referring to man-made religious ideas that are not based on the Word of God. Our Lord rejected man's religious traditions (Mark 7:1-13). Paul warned against them in Colossians 2:8. It is sad to see religious people argue over man's traditions and, at the same time, reject the simple truth of the Word of God.

The word *tradition* simply means "that which is handed down from one person to another." The truth of the Gospel began as an oral message proclaimed by Christ and the apostles. Later, this truth was written down by the inspiration of the Holy Spirit, and it became Holy Scripture (see 2 Tim. 3:12-17 and 2 Peter 2:16-21). God's truth was not invented by men: it was handed down from God to man (Gal. 1:11-12; 1 Cor. 15:1-6); and each generation of believers had guarded this truth and passed it on to others (2 Tim. 2:2).

Paul stated clearly the believers' dual responsibility in guarding the truth: "stand fast, and hold the traditions" (2 Thes. 2:15). *Stand fast* means, "Do not move away from the truth of the Gospel" (see 1 Cor. 16:13 and Col. 1:23). When my wife and I visited the Tower of London and saw the royal jewels, we noticed that the crowd was kept moving, but the guards stood still. They were constantly watching the visitors and nothing could move them from their appointed places. You and I are helping to guard the "precious faith" and we must not be moved by the wiles of Satan or the praises of men.

If we *stand*, then we can *hold*. This word means "to hold fast, to hold firmly." It is related to a Greek word that means "strength, might, power." We are not to hold God's truth in a careless way, but grasp it firmly with power and never let it slip from us. Each generation of Christians must receive the truth from others, guard it, and make sure it is kept intact for the next generation.

It is not easy to *stand* and *hold*, because forces around us want to move us from the faith. Satan knows how to use lies to oppose God's truth, and he seeks to do this *within the fellowship* (Acts 20:28-32). Sometimes faithful believers must refuse the fellowship of those who have rejected the faith

(Rom. 16:17-20; 2 Cor. 6:14—7:1; 2 John 7-10; 1 Tim. 6:3-5).

Let me sum this up with two words of caution. First, "the faith" that has been handed down to us must not be confused with man's interpretations and ideas. The Pharisees made their own interpretations as sacred as the Word of God (Mark 7:7-9). The basic doctrines of God's Word are held by all evangelical believers, but not all believers agree on minor matters of interpretation (especially in the area of prophecy) or matters of church order. It is dangerous to make man's ideas a test of fellowship or spirituality.

Second, we must not embalm the truth so that it loses its life and power. We are to be like faithful householders who bring out of God's treasury of truth "things new and old" (Matt. 13:52). There is yet more truth to be found in God's Word, and we must not think that we know it all. The Word is like seed (Luke 8:11), and when seed is sown, it produces plants, fruit, *and more seed.* While it is good to "tell the old, old story" it is also good to let the Spirit teach us new truths from the Word, and to make new applications of old truths.

Practice the Truth (2:16-17)

It is not enough to believe the truth and guard it; we must also practice it. If we hear the Word, but do not obey it, we are only fooling ourselves (James 1:22-25).

These two verses record Paul's desire and prayer for his friends: he wanted God to *encourage* them ("comfort your hearts") and *establish* them ("stablish you") "in every good word and work." Both of these words are prominent in the Thessalonian letters.

When Paul was with them, he *encouraged* them individually as a father does his children (1 Thes. 2:11). He sent Timothy to encourage them (3:2), and Paul himself was greatly encouraged with Timothy's report of their faithfulness (3:7).

Paul encouraged them to walk to please God (4:1), and to grow in their love for others (4:10). He taught them about the rapture of the church in order that they might encourage each other (4:18). To calm their fears, he explained the Day of the Lord to them (5:11). In addition to his teaching, he urged them to minister to each other (5:18).

Establishment in the Lord is also an important theme. Paul sent Timothy back to Thessalonica that he might establish them in their faith (1 Thes. 3:2); and Paul prayed that God might establish them (3:13). The child must be taught to stand before he can learn to walk or run.

It is God who establishes, but He uses people to accomplish His work. A great need in our churches is for Christians who will take time to establish the younger believers. Group Bible studies are very valuable, as are the public meetings of the church; but individual discipling is also important. Paul encouraged the Thessalonican believers on a one-to-one basis, and we should follow his example.

Paul was concerned about two aspects of their Christian life: their *word* and their *work*, their *saying* and their *doing*. If our walk contradicts our words, we lose our testimony. Our "walk" and our "talk" must agree; good works and good words must come from the same yielded heart.

We are not saved by good works (Titus 3:3-7; Eph. 2:8-10); but good works are the evidence of salvation (Titus 2:11-15). It is not enough to depend on good words; the words must be backed up by the deeds (1 John 3:18). It must be a steady practice, not an occasional one. We must be *established* in our words and works.

How is this possible? Only God can do it by His grace; and this is what Paul desired for his friends. God has given us eternal encouragement and good hope through His grace. Notice that Paul's words united the Lord Jesus Christ and God the Father in such a way that he affirmed the deity of Christ. The two names for God in verse 16 are governed by a *singular* verb, not a plural, which means they are equal. He used the same construction in 1 Thessalonians 3:11, again affirming the equality of the Son with the Father.

Too many Christians today emphasize *guarding* the truth, but downplay *living* the truth. One of the best ways to guard the truth is to put it into practice. It is good to be defenders of the faith, but we must not forget to he demonstrators of the faith. Lazarus did not have to give lectures on the resurrection. People had only to look at him and they believed (John 2:9-11).

Share the Truth (3:1-5)

A sequence of responsibilities is logical. Learning and living must go together. If we believe the truth, it changes our lives. We guard the truth and practice it so that we can share it with others. We cannot share what we do not believe (unless we want to be hypocrites); and we can best share that which we have practiced ourselves.

God's Word is alive (Heb. 4:12); we must let it move freely. Paul alluded here to Psalm 147:15— "He sent forth His commandment upon earth: His word runneth very swiftly." God's servants may be bound, but God's Word cannot be bound (2 Tim. 2:9). As we practice the truth and pray for the ministry of the truth, God's Word will have freedom to run and accomplish God's purposes in the world.

The Word of God is glorified in the lives of those who share it and those who receive it. This was Paul's experience in Antioch of Pisidia: "And when the Gentiles heard this [that they could be saved], they were glad, and glorified the Word of the Lord: and as many as were ordained to eternal life believed. And the Word of the Lord was published [spread abroad] throughout all the region" (Acts 13:48-49).

Too much Christian work these days is accomplished by human plans and promotion, and not by the Word of God. We trust our programs and do not publish the Word of God. We publish our programs and also do not trust the Word of God. The universe was created, and is sustained, by the Word of God (Heb. 11:3). Surely His Word can accomplish His work in this world. But the preaching of the Word in the pulpit has too often been replaced by the entertainment of the world on the platform. Dr. Donald Coggan, Archbishop of Canterbury, has said of Christian pastors: "It is their task to feed the sheep—not to entertain the goats."

It has been my experience in three pastorates that God's Word will accomplish God's work. When the sheep are fed, they will flock together in love, reproduce, follow the shepherd—and they can be "fleeced" and will love it. It is when the sheep are hungry that they start biting each other, becoming sick, and wandering away. When the Word of God does the work, then God gets the glory. My good friend Dr. Bob Cook used to remind us, "If you can explain what is going on, then God isn't doing it!"

Of course, there is always opposition to the Word and work of God. Paul asked his friends to pray that he might be delivered from unbelieving men who were evil and wicked. Just as the Spirit uses dedicated people to share the Word, Satan uses wicked people to oppose the Word. The evil one enjoys using Christian believers to oppose the work of God. He spoke through Peter (Matt. 16:21-23), and he worked through Ananias and Sapphira (Acts 5:1-11).

Paul had confidence that his readers would not yield to Satan, but would permit the faithful Lord to establish them and guard them from the evil one (literal meaning of 3:3). We cannot have confidence in ourselves, but we can have confidence in God for ourselves and for others.

It is not enough that the pastor or church officers alone share the Word; each Christian must be a part of this vital ministry. The word *command* that Paul used in 3:4 means "a military order passed down from a superior officer." He used this word in 1 Thessalonians 4:2; and he repeated it in this chapter in verses 4, 6, 10, 12. Christ is the Captain of our Salvation; we are His soldiers (2 Tim. 2:3-4). In a battle, it is not enough for only the officers to fight; every man must do his duty. This is also true in the work of the local church.

What if an army were run with the same lack of obedience, order, and discipline that we often see in the local church? It would never win the war. If soldiers attended drill whenever they felt like it, they would never be equipped to face the enemy. If the recruits disobeyed their officers' orders the way some church members disobey the Word of God, they would be court-martialed.

A soldier obeys primarily out of loyalty and fear. But a Christian has much higher motives for obedience: God's love and Christ's return (v. 5). "If ye love Me, keep My commandments" (John 14:15). A commanding officer does not require his men to love him; but if they do, they will respect and obey him with greater diligence. The history of warfare records heroic deeds done by men who loved their leaders and willingly died for them. Our Saviour loved us and died for us. Can we not obey Him?

He is coming for us. This has been the theme of Paul's two letters to the Thessalonicans, and he related this truth to everyday practical living. As God's soldiers, we must be sharing the Word, for He will one day return and ask for an accounting of our lives. Do we "love His appearing"? (2 Tim. 4:8) Will we "be ashamed before Him at His coming"? (1 John 2:28)

Here, then are four great responsibilities for us to fulfill: believe the truth, guard the truth, practice the truth, and share the truth. If we fulfill these duties, we will experience joy and power in our lives, and growth and blessing in our churches.

⁶Now we command you, brethren, in the name of our Lord Jesus Christ, that ye withdraw yourselves from every brother that walketh disorderly, and not after the tradition which he received of us. ⁷For yourselves know how ye ought to follow us: for we behaved not ourselves disorderly among you; ⁸neither did we eat any man's bread for nought; but wrought with labor and travail night and day, that we might not be chargeable to any of you: ⁹not because we have not power, but to make ourselves an example unto you to follow us. ¹⁰For even when we were with you, this we commanded you, that if any would not work, neither should he eat. ¹¹For we hear that there are some which walk among you disorderly, working not at all, but are busybodies. ¹²Now them that are such we command and exhort by our Lord Jesus Christ, that with quietness they work, and eat their own bread. ¹³But ye, brethren, be not weary in well-doing. ¹⁴And if any man obey not our word by this epistle, note that man, and have no company with him, that he may be ashamed. ¹⁵Yet count him not as an enemy, but admonish him as a brother. ¹⁶Now the Lord of peace Himself give you peace always by all means. The Lord be with you all. ¹⁷The salutation of Paul with mine own hand, which is the token in every epistle: so I write. ¹⁸The grace of our Lord Jesus Christ be with you all. Amen.

2 Thessalonians 3:6-18

13
Order
in the Church

When problems are not solved, they grow and become worse. A sliver left in the finger can become infected and cause a toxic condition so serious that surgery may become necessary. If you tell your doctor that you stepped on a rusty nail, he will immediately give you a tetanus shot, even though the wound may appear insignificant to you.

Church problems are like physical problems: if left unsolved, they grow and become worse, and they infect more people. The local church is a body; and what germs are to the physical body, sin is to the spiritual body. When Paul wrote his first letter to the Thessalonican church, he warned the idle busybodies to get to work (1 Thes. 4:11). He admonished the church leaders to "warn them that are unruly" (5:14). The word "unruly" means "a soldier out of rank." Apparently these troublemakers did not repent, because Paul devoted the rest of his second letter to this problem.

What was the problem? Some members of the assembly had misinterpreted Paul's teachings about the return of Christ, left their jobs, and were living off the generosity of the church. They were idle while others were working. Yet they expected the church to support them. It is possible that this group of lazy saints was the source of the false teaching Paul mentioned in 2 Thessalonians 2:2. They were also spreading gossip about people in the church. They had time on their hands and gossip on their lips, but they defended themselves by arguing, "The Lord is coming soon!"

Misinterpretations and misapplications of the truths of God's Word can cause endless trouble History records the foolishness of people who set dates, sold their possessions, and sat on mountains waiting for the Lord to return. Any teaching that encourages us to disobey another divine teaching is not Bible teaching.

The Pharisees figured out a way to rob their parents and yet obey the fifth commandment:

And He (Jesus) said to them, "Rightly did Isaiah prophesy of you hypocrites, as it is written, 'This people honors Me with their lips, but their heart is far away from Me. But in vain do they worship Me, teaching as doctrines the precepts of men.' Neglecting the commandment of God, you hold to the tradition of men." He was also saying to them, "You nicely set aside the commandment of God in order to keep your tradition. For Moses said, 'Honor your father and your mother;' and 'He who speaks evil of father or mother, let him be put to death;' but you say, 'If a man says to his father or his mother, anything of mine you might have been helped by is Corban (that is to say, given to God),'

you no longer permit him to do anything for
his father or his mother; thus invalidating the
word of God by your tradition which you
have handed down; and you do many such
things like that" (Mark 7:6-13, NASB).

Paul expected the whole church to work together in solving this problem. The church in love
must deal with its own members and seek to help
each one obey God. To assist them in this task,
Paul gave four motives to encourage the careless
believers to turn from their sins and start earning
their own bread.

The Exhortation of the Word (3:6)
Paul had used this powerful word *command* in his
first Thessalonian letter (4:2, 11); and we met it
earlier in this chapter (v. 4). He used it again
in verses 10 and 12. The word means "a military
order handed down from a superior officer." Paul
considered the church to be like an army; and if
the army does not obey the orders, there can be no
order. Unfortunately, some of the saints were "out
of rank" ("unruly" in 1 Thes. 5:14, and "disorderly"
in 2 Thes. 3:6, 7 and 11).

What authority did Paul have to issue this command, "If any is not willing to work, neither should
he eat"? (v. 10, literal translation) He had the
authority of the name of the Lord Jesus Christ. At
least 20 times in the Thessalonian letters, Paul used
this complete title of the Saviour. *Jesus* means
"Saviour" and is His human name (Matt. 1:21).
Christ is His divine title; it means "Messiah—the
Anointed One." Other persons could use the name
Jesus (the Hebrew form is "Joshua"); and other
persons could claim to be anointed, such as

prophets, priests, and kings. But the two names, Jesus Christ, are further defined by the name *LORD*, "Jehovah God."

In the four Gospels and the Book of Acts, our Lord is often called Jesus; but this single name is used very infrequently in the rest of the New Testament. That it is *occasionally* used should restrain us from criticizing those who call their Saviour "Jesus"; but that its use is found mainly during His ministry on earth should encourage us to address Him, and speak of Him with His name of exaltation—Lord Jesus Christ (Phil. 2:11). We no longer know "Christ after the flesh" (2 Cor. 5:16), but as the exalted Son of God and "Head over all things to the church." His Lordship includes our work and money management.

What does the Bible teach about manual (or mental) labor? For one thing, labor was a part of man's life *before* sin entered the scene. God gave Adam the job of dressing and guarding the Garden (Gen. 2:15). Although sin turned labor into almost hopeless toil (Gen. 3:17-19), it must never be thought that the necessity for work is a result of sin. Man needs work for the fulfillment of his own person. God created him to work.

Have you noticed that God called people who were busy at work? Moses was caring for sheep (Ex. 3). Joshua was Moses' servant before he became Moses' successor (Ex. 33:11). Gideon was threshing wheat when God called him (Jud. 6:11ff), and David was caring for his father's sheep (1 Sam. 16:11ff). Our Lord called four fishermen to serve as His disciples, and He Himself had worked as a carpenter. Paul was a tentmaker (Acts 18:1-3) and used his trade to support his own ministry.

The Jews honored honest labor and required all their rabbis to have a trade. But the Greeks despised manual labor and left it to their slaves. This Greek influence, plus their wrong ideas about the doctrine of the Lord's return, led these believers into an unchristian way of life.

Paul recognized the fact that some people could not work, perhaps because of physical handicaps or family responsibilities. This is why he phrased the statement as he did: "If any man *is not willing* to work." It was not a question of *ability* but *willingness*. When a believer cannot work and is in need, it is the privilege and duty of the church to help him (James 2:14-17; 1 John 3:16-18).

The exhortation of the Word should have motivated these lazy believers to work; but Paul added a second motivation.

The Example of the Apostle (3:7-10)

As an apostle, Paul had the right to expect financial support; but he deliberately gave up this right that he might be an example to the young believers (see 1 Cor. 9:6-14). In this attitude, Paul proved himself to be a mature Christian leader. Selfish leaders use people to build up their support, and they are always claiming their rights. A truly dedicated leader will use his rights to build up the people, and will lay aside his rights and privileges for the sake of others.

He had referred to his example in labor in his previous letter (1 Thes. 2:9). His readers knew that Paul and his associates had not taken any support from the infant church. Instead, they had set the example of meeting their own needs and also helping to meet the needs of others. "You ought to imitate us," he admonished his readers.

The greatest influence is that of godly living and sacrifice. A Christian leader may appeal to the authority of the Word; but if he cannot point also to his own example of obedience, his people will not listen. This is the difference between *authority* and *stature*. A leader earns stature as he obeys the Word and serves His people in the will of God. Authority comes from position; stature comes from practice and example. Stature earns the leader the right to exercise authority.

Every Christian worker has the right to support from the church as he serves the Lord (Luke 10:7; Gal. 6:6; 1 Tim. 5:17-18). We must not use Paul's example as an excuse not to support God's servants. But any servant of God has the privilege of setting aside that right to the glory of God. Paul did this so that he might be an example to the young believers in Thessalonica.

Paul's policy not only encouraged the new believers but also silenced the accusers. In every city there were itinerant teachers who "peddled their wares" for what they could earn. Paul did not want to be classified with them. Nor did he want any unsaved person to say, "Paul preaches only to make money." As he stated in 1 Corinthians 9, Paul wanted to make the Gospel "free of charge;" he would not permit money to hinder the winning of lost souls.

Needless to say, the careless attitude of these believers was affecting the church; so Paul added yet a third motive for their obedience.

The Encouragement of the Church (3:11-15)

Verse 13 is the key: "And you, brothers, do not lose heart doing good!" (literal translation) The

faithful Christians were discouraged by the conduct of the careless saints who refused to work.
"If *they* don't have to work, why should *we?*" was
their argument; and Paul nipped it in the bud.

Sin in the life of a believer always affects the
rest of the church. As members of His body, we
belong to each other and we affect each other. The
bad example of a few saints can destroy the devotion, and hinder the service, of the rest of the
church.

Paul named the sins of this group. To begin
with, they were "disorderly," or out of order, out
of rank. They were disobeying orders, and this
brought confusion and division to the assembly.
Further, they were "busybodies," not busy workers.
The Greek word for "busybody" literally means "to
be working around"; that is, busy but "fooling
around" and not accomplishing anything. First
Timothy 5:13 suggests that busybodies meddle in
matters that do not belong to them.

Almost every culture has its saying about idle-
ness. The Romans said, "By doing nothing, men
learn to do evil." Isaac Watts wrote: "For Satan
finds some mischief still, for idle hands to do." The
Jewish rabbis taught, "He who does not teach his
son a trade, teaches him to be a thief."

Instead of noisily running around, these people
should "with quietness . . . work, and eat their
own bread." Their false views about the return
of Christ had worked them into a pitch of excite-
ment. "Your overemotional attitude is wrong,"
warned Paul. "Settle down and get to work." Work
is a great antidote to unbalanced speculation and
unthinking activity.

But suppose these saints did *not* obey God's
Word and go to work? What then should the

church do? Paul had already taken the first step when he exhorted them in his first letter (1 Thes. 5:14) and warned them that they were wrong. But they had still persisted in their unruly behavior. He now warned them again in his second letter, and then added a further step: if these believers did not obey, the members of the church should personally discipline them.

The subject of church discipline is not discussed much these days. In many churches, once a person is baptized and becomes a member of a local church, he is pretty much left to himself. If he commits some gross public sin, he will probably be dealt with by the pastor or the board; but the total church family will not begin to minister to him or exercise discipline over him.

What is church discipline? For one thing, it is *not* the pastor and official board acting like evangelical policemen to trap a sinning saint and kick him out of the church. No doubt there are churches that have such dictatorial leaders, but this is not what Paul had in mind. Church discipline is to the church member what family discipline is to a child: it is an exercise of, and evidence of, correcting love. When a parent disciplines his child, it is not a judge punishing a criminal; it is a loving father seeking to make his child a better person.

There are various levels of church discipline that must be distinguished.

1. Personal differences between Christians (Matt. 18:15-18; Phil. 4:1-3). If a brother or sister sins against me (either deliberately or unknowingly), I should go to that person privately and seek to get the matter settled. Only if the person refuses to settle the matter should I bring anyone else in; and the problem must not go to the church family until every other means has been exhausted.

In my pastoral ministry, I have seen many problems of this type. The big mistake Christians make when another believer wrongs them is in telling the pastor or other members, and not going to the person directly. Another mistake is in trying to win an argument instead of trying to win the sinning brother.

2. *Doctrinal error.* Determine first of all why the person is teaching wrong doctrine. Perhaps it is because of ignorance and lack of Bible knowledge. In that case, patiently teach him the truth (2 Tim. 2:23-26). If he persists, rebuke him (Titus 1:10-14). Paul had to do this to Peter (Gal. 2:11ff). If the error continues, avoid him (Rom. 16:17-18), and then separate yourself from him (2 Tim. 2:18ff; 2 John 9ff).

3. *A believer overtaken by sin (Gal. 6:1-3).* Even the great Apostle Peter denied the Lord. And David yielded to lust and committed adultery. When a Christian is caught in known sin, the spiritual members of the church must seek to restore him with gentleness and love. The word *restore* here means "to set a broken bone"—and that takes tenderness and patience. Too often the church quickly passes judgment on a believer who has sinned, and the damage done causes problems for years to come.

4. *A repeating troublemaker (Titus 3:10).* The word *heretic* does not refer to doctrinal error, but to a proud attitude of one who gets people to "take sides" in the church. The Greek word means "to make a choice." This leads to divisions and cliques in the local church (See Gal. 5:20 where *heresies* ought to be translated "sects, parties.") There is hardly a church that does not have its parties *for* or

against anything—the pastor, the building program,
even the color of the kitchen walls. Usually these
"heretics" are people who like to be important; they
want a following. Often they have deep emotional
problems that Satan can use to create spiritual
problems in the church. Perhaps they are frustrated at home, or on the job; or perhaps they
have, in the past, been hurt by some pastor or
church.

These "factious people" should be given two
official warnings. If they repeat their sin of divid-
ing the church, they should be given a third warning and rejected. "Warn a divisive person once, and
then warn him a second time. After that, have
nothing to do with him. You may be sure that such
a man is warped and sinful; he is self-condemned"
(Titus 3:10-11, NIV).

It is my conviction that such people should not
hold office in the church. It is also my conviction
that, if they leave the church "in a huff," they
should be restored to fellowship only twice. The
third time—they are out!

5. *Open immorality (1 Cor. 5).* The church must
mourn over the sinner (the same word is used for
mourning over the dead) and seek to bring him
to repentance. If he refuses, the church collectively
should dismiss him (v. 13, where the Greek word
means "expel"). If he repents, he must be forgiven
and restored to fellowship in the church (2 Cor.
2:6-11).

In the case of the "lazy saints," Paul told the
believers to exhort them, warn them, and if they
did not repent, withdraw intimate fellowship from
them. This probably meant that these believers
were not permitted to share in the Lord's Supper,
and that the church members would not invite

them to their homes. Second Thessalonians 3:14 does *not* apply to every case of discipline. It applies only to the matter of saints not working for a living.

"Have no company" literally means "do not get mixed up with;" the same word is used in 1 Corinthians 5:9. There is a difference between acquaintanceship, friendship, and fellowship; for fellowship means "to have in common." For obedient saints to treat disobedient Christians with the same friendship they show to other dedicated saints is to give approval to their sins.

However, Paul (knowing the tendency of human nature to go to extremes) cautioned them not to treat the offenders like enemies. "They are still your brothers in Christ," he added. Lot was out of fellowship with God and Abraham because he lived in Sodom; yet Abraham rescued Lot from the enemy because Lot was his brother (Gen. 14, and note especially v. 14). It requires much patience, love, and grace to help an erring brother; and this is why Paul added a final motive for earning a living.

The Enablement of the Lord (3:16-18)

No believer can say, "I am not able to obey God's Word and go to work," because God has made every provision for us to obey Him. He is the Lord of peace. If He is the Lord of our lives, then we will have peace in our own hearts, and we will help to encourage peace in our church fellowship.

If there is trouble in the church, it is because there is trouble in somebody's heart. If Christ is Lord, then there is peace in the heart. If there is war in the heart, then Jesus Christ is not Lord. (See James 4:1-10.)

I recall a Sunday School class that was in a constant state of confusion and competition. We would just get matters settled down for a few weeks when the volcano would erupt again. After much prayer and examination, we discovered that one class member wanted to be the teacher. She was proud of her own spiritual attainments and felt she could do a better job than the devoted lady who was teaching the class.

Even though this class member never openly attacked or criticized the teacher, her attitudes and the things she did *not* say sowed seeds of discord in the fellowship. When this problem was dealt with, the Lord of peace took over in the class, and God began to bless.

Not only does God's peace enable us to obey Him, but so does His presence: "The Lord be with you all!" He never leaves us or forsakes us; He is with us to the end of the age (Heb. 13:5; Matt. 28:20).

Finally, Paul reminded them of God's grace. "The grace of our Lord Jesus Christ be with you all" (v. 18) was Paul's official signature to his letters. He mentioned this because of the counterfeit letter they had received (2 Thes. 2:2). If we depend on the grace of God, we can do His will to the glory of God. "My grace is sufficient for thee" (2 Cor. 12:9).

The soldier who is out of rank and disobedient to the Lord's command proves that he is not surrendered to his Master. Church problems are individual problems, and they must be solved individually. God wants order in the church. "Let all things be done decently and in order" (1 Cor. 14:40).

Are you a part of the peace of the church or

part of a war in the church?

Let's do what Joshua did and fall at the feet of the Captain of the Hosts of the Lord, that He might enable us to win the victory (Josh. 5:13-15), and fulfill His purposes for His people.

The Lord is coming soon. BE READY!